FOR D.T. VALENTINE'S MANUAL 1856

MEADOWS
St. Nicholas Hotel Broadway
PSON 1735

TOMAHAWKS TO TEXTILES

Lake Manahatta, the historic Indian lake that supplied fresh water to Manhattan Island for more than a thousand years.

Tomahawks to Textiles

The Fabulous Story of Worth Street

by

FRANK L. WALTON

APPLETON-CENTURY-CROFTS, INC.

New York

The poem "Worth Village" by Floyd W. Jefferson is
reproduced by the kind permission of the author.

WORTH VILLAGE

Within the confines of these age-old streets
Where, years agone, in solemn grandeur stood,
New York's great Hospital of Charity,
There moves today a friendly brotherhood.
Here is the Gateway to the Worth Street mart,
World famous, honored textile trading post,
Where verbal contracts are a sacred pledge
Where word is bond, integrity the boast.
Worth, Leonard, Franklin, White and Thomas streets,
On West and East by Church and Broadway bound,
Blocks of tradition where there breathes a soul,
Where, clothed in pride, time-honored names are found.
A guest or stranger in the Merchants Club,
Where all the speech is this or that per cent,
Is shown John Preston's portrait on the stairs,
Inscribed with mystic words, "Sell and Repent."

Worth Village rises where the Indians roamed,
Near Collect Pond, a great fresh-water lake,
Where Sachems bartered land for golden guilders   -
With rich Manhattan Island as the stake.
Though far removed from Southland's sunny clime,
Before our eyes a misty mirage looms,
We see the factories with spindles whirling,
The spreading fields with snow-white cotton blooms,
The mansion house, green lawns and porticos,
Fair ladies in their spotless crinoline,
Lord of the manor with his frosted glass,
And old black Joe, complete the happy scene.
The mirage fades. Back in the world of men,
Back in old Worth Street's busy port of trade
We live and laugh and love in amity,
Our shoulders blessed with knighthood's accolade.
Community with soul and vibrant heart,
The fairest business realm in all the earth,
Where friend greets friend in very verity,
Long life and honor to the Village Worth.

FLOYD W. JEFFERSON

The Purpose of This Book

Most people are interested in history—in the happenings of long ago. Almost everyone is inclined to reminisce about the old country, the old home town, or about the things that happened in his childhood or in the early days of his business career, for all these things have left memories that will be carried throughout life.

There is a strange fascination about old places, old legends, and old history. It intrigues the imagination to recall human experiences and to link them together, for somehow the past seems to offer a background against which to view the present and the future.

It is not difficult to write the history of a residential community, for people, their families and their homes, set the stage for a human-interest story. The story of a business community, however, particularly one that is only a part of a larger business area set in a huge metropolis, offers a greater challenge, even though the district is made up of many personalities—men and women—who have a community of interest in their work.

The inspiration for this story comes from the fine community spirit in the Worth Street District of New York City, developed over a period of many years and built very largely around a pioneering spirit, a common interest of people in textiles and their belief that textiles have a mission in the world—a mission to serve humanity. It seems safe to assume that there is no other business district just like it in any city, large or small.

We are indebted to many sources for the historical data recorded here and to many people for specific information, which is duly acknowledged. Particular credit is due to John L. Severance for his great assistance and to A. B. Carlson of the New-York Historical Society for his interest and help with maps, pictures and historical data.

FRANK L. WALTON

Foreword

Worth Village is situated in the heart of New York City. Bounded by Chambers and Canal Streets, West Broadway, the Bowery and Park Row, it occupies the site of Manahatta —the Indian village out of which grew the fabulous city of today.

Long before 1609, when Henry Hudson sailed into the river which now bears his name, there was an Indian Manhattan in which the present-day amenities of New York flourished in a simple form.

There was significance in the name the Indians originally gave this place—"Manahatin"—"manah" meaning island, and "atin" meaning hill. What is now known as the island of Manhattan was then really two islands—a northern and a southern island. Manahatta, built on the shores of a lake, was on the southern island.

For more than three centuries men have changed the face but not the spirit of the Manahatta of the Indians and its direct successor, Worth Village.

Before Hudson came, the Indians traded here among themselves. The men who followed Hudson were traders rather than colonists, and the fine harbor was to their liking. They were tradesmen before they were industrialists, and merchants before they were bankers.

The greatness of Manhattan today is no accident. The Indians were drawn to the site of Manahatta because of its advantages: a lake of fresh water on a rocky island surrounded by salt water. The white men for more than three centuries were attracted by the opportunities offered—opportunities found nowhere else in the world.

Worth Village takes its name from its "main street"—
Worth Street. It is a street, or district, which is known through-
out the world as the greatest of textile centers. It originally
bore the name of Catherine Street, in honor of the wife of
Hendricks Rutgers, who once owned a farm near what is now
Chatham Square. In 1803 the name was changed to Anthony
Street. In 1855 it received its present name in honor of Brevet
Major General William Jenkins Worth, a famous officer of the
Mexican War.

While the name Worth goes back less than a century, the
village history goes back to the very founding of Manahatta
by the Indians. A century ago the textile merchants of New
York began to concentrate in this area, and soon it became
known as the textile hub of the world.

Worth Village is the primary market through which the
products of the mills reach the consumers. In the early days
a good part of the textiles produced by the mills were shipped
to the firms in Worth Street, the goods actually being handled
there before being distributed.

In recent years, as business has increased and transportation and distribution methods have improved, most of the
goods have been shipped from the mills direct to the buyers.
But the men and firms of Worth Street still act as the clearinghouse for hundreds of textile mills in New England and the
South by handling the sales, and in general, the advertising,
invoicing and credits necessary to a wide distribution of the
products. There are also other firms in Worth Village. Some
buy goods from these primary market firms, some convert
goods and some represent customers located in various sections of the country. There are textile bankers, also brokers,
wholesalers and other distributors. They all play an important
part in making Worth Street what it is today.

Worth Street firms sell most of the cloth produced in the
United States from cotton grown on more than twenty million
acres of cotton land stretching under the Southern sun from
Virginia to California. The Street is also a great market place

for cloth manufactured from man-made fibers such as rayon. It is a place where woolen goods are sold, as well as flaxen fabrics, and cloth woven from fibers derived from mineral sources, such as glass fiber and nylon.

A tremendous responsibility rests upon the men and firms of Worth Street, for they are the link between millions of people who depend for their livelihood upon the growth, production and processing of fibers, and the other millions who buy and use the products.

Amid the activity of the present, it is well to pause and contemplate the past, for from its past Worth Street and Worth Village can take great courage and assurance for the future.

The story of Worth Street as a textile center goes back only one century. But this story, in turn, is built upon the early story of Manhattan—in fact the historical story of the Worth Street area *is* the foundation story of Manhattan.

This year—1953—is being celebrated as the three hundredth anniversary of the incorporation of New York as a city, but three centuries represent only a small part of the history of Manhattan and Worth Village.

Behind the less than three and one-half centuries of written history which began when Hudson arrived in 1609, Manhattan has another three thousand years of unwritten history— the story of the Indians, who left no books, maps or written documents, but who passed their story down in legends and artifacts.

The story goes back even farther than the Indians. The millions of people who daily rush about Manhattan probably never think of the time when there were no human beings on the island—thousands and millions of years ago, when nature was preparing the site.

The story of Worth Village—the original Manahatta—and the men of Worth who today transact business there, is a fascinating one. Nowhere else in the world could such a story be found, just as there is no other Manhattan.

Contents

Chapter I

The Emergence of Manhattan

Man is no longer satisfied to regard the little world around him as the universe, nor is he content to look upon a few hundred—or a few thousand—years of written history as the complete story of himself and the earth upon which he lives. He realizes that great forces are at work in nature—inexorable forces—and that constant changes are taking place: changes that have been at work through ages and eras reckoned by geologists in millions of years.

New Yorkers often forget this, and the history that is recorded in the rocks upon which they have built their city. In a span of three centuries they have filled in streams and lakes, carved highways and streets out of forests and then destroyed the forests. They have bored into the rocks for their subways and have erected tall buildings. But they seldom pause to think what was here before man himself.

Not so long ago as time is counted in geology, possibly ten million years, the whole northeastern part of the American continent was a mile higher than it now is. Manhattan, then not even an island, was a link in a long chain of rugged hills that extended several hundred miles farther out into the ocean. The Hudson River flowed down its valley to the west of this plateau. The Connecticut River flowed through a valley now covered by Long Island Sound, and through what is now the East River, until it joined the Hudson. The Hudson River at that time entered the Atlantic at a point far distant from its present mouth. Even today, a wide dark streak on the ocean floor can be seen from an airplane. This is the old channel,

which sank beneath the Atlantic when the land surface settled
to its present level.

There had been a time when the Hudson River itself had not
existed. In the dim geological past there was an upthrust of
hard rock that formed two almost perpendicular barriers of
solid granite. Today one wall is the Palisades, the west bank
of the Hudson. The other wall, steep in some places but
rounded at the top in others, is now the east bank of the
Hudson. These two walls of granite formed a trough about a
mile wide and a half-mile or so deep, which by some quirk
of nature was filled with a deposit of softer rock, or shale. In
time, the elements caused this softer rock to deteriorate, and
the particles disappeared into the ocean as the rains and melt-
ing snows formed first a trickling brook, later a larger stream
and finally a mighty river. These palisaded walls today vary in
height from one hundred to five hundred feet above water
level, and are an ever-present example of nature's unyielding
law that nothing shall be permanent. Nature has a way of
building up and tearing down—a process of leveling off. When
the granite walls that now confine the Hudson, particularly the
western shore, are examined, the rubble at the base gives mute
evidence that even now the Palisades, one of the wonders of
nature, are slowly but surely being eroded away.

Eventually a great disturbance within the regions of the
earth caused the plateau or mountain chain of which Manhattan was a part to settle down. The ocean moved in to fill
the low places. The lower portion of the Hudson disappeared
under the sea, while a portion of the Connecticut River sank
under the waters of what is now Long Island Sound. The sea
rushed in through a break in the mountain chain to form a
waterway which is now the Harlem River. An island was
formed—the island to become known as Manhattan. Actually,
two islands were formed, because farther south, at a point
which is now a route marked by Canal and Roosevelt Streets,
water filled another cut in the mountain chain.

In the fullness of time the two islands grew greener. Their

surfaces, broken here and there by rocky hills, took on a covering of grasses and shrubs, which thrived on the accumulated glacial soil. In the deeper pockets trees took root, and their falling leaves helped build more soil to cover the land, and as the soil grew deeper and the trees reproduced themselves the slender trees grew into mighty forests.

Land life appeared and developed through these formative years. Small animals and then larger ones made their homes in the sheltered areas. Birds appeared and in their flights spread seeds, playing their part in the growth of vegetation. In time the islands, especially the southern one, became animal havens. Trails began to appear on the surface as these animals moved from place to place seeking food and fresh water.

The center of attraction of this island paradise was a great fresh-water lake situated at the northern extremity of the southern island. Most of the animals of the two islands visited this lake at one time or another. When winter froze the small springs and streams, or drought dried up their sources, the fresh-water lake supplied their needs, for it was sixty feet deep —an immense bowl formed in the solid rock, with its wide basin covering several hundred acres. The southern island thus became a refuge as well as a center for the animal world, and all trails led to the fresh-water lake that was eventually to play such an important role in the history of Manhattan and of Worth Village.

Approaching Canal Street today along Broadway or Lafayette, it is difficult to realize that this wide paved thoroughfare was once part of a salt-water passage cutting the present-day island of Manhattan into two islands. As late as the latter part of the Indian era and the early part of the Dutch era there are legendary accounts of this salt-water route, which was used by the Indians in going to and from their village on the lake. There are also references to high tides which at one time swept into the waterway from both the Hudson and the East Rivers and met in the middle.

A study of the geological maps of the Canal Street area

shows that the rock formation is from fifty to one hundred feet below the present land surface and well below the levels of the Hudson and East Rivers—evidence that at one time there was indeed a deep natural waterway separating the two islands, and that the action of the tides in forcing water from both rivers into the passage caused an eddy and the gradual accumulation of silt. By the time the Dutch arrived the passage had become largely a swamp, with small streams of fresh water passing west and east down its center. One of these streams flowed through the swamp to the Hudson, and was named Lapinikan Creek after the Indian settlement at its mouth. The other, known as Old Wreck Creek, flowed to the East River. An old map, which appears in the map section of this book, clearly outlines the swamp, the two streams and the lake.

The swamp to the west was first drained in 1748, when a small canal was cut to the Hudson. In 1800, a plan was widely discussed to dredge this water route across the island to restore the old salt-water passage so that ships might reach the lake, which would then become a safe harbor for shipping, away from the tides that plagued small vessels anchored in the two large rivers. If this had been done, Manhattan might today be two islands. However, the project fell through, and by 1810 Canal Street was laid out and in 1819 the canal covered over. By this action the two islands became one, at least on the surface. But the historic stream still flows through an aqueduct beneath the street.

CHAPTER II

The Indians Arrive

The American Indians were the first known inhabitants of the American continent, and they developed a civilization of their own. The early history of the race is clothed in the fog of antiquity, but its civilization dates back many thousands of years. There are Indian legends in which they speak of their ancestors' migrating to the east from the banks of "the great waters." Whether the legendary area was the Pacific Ocean or an inland sea may never be known.

In their trek to the east, the Indian tribes were seeking the Rising Sun. To them it represented the supernatural—either the god of whom their legends spoke, or the light which their god turned on them to see what they were doing.

Seeking the paradise of the Rising Sun, a number of tribes crossed the plains of what is now New York State and arrived at the shores of a majestic river. Some felt they had reached their haven, and settled there. Others felt the urge to follow on to the east, and continued into what is now New England.

And there were still other tribes, fascinated by the mighty river, which they named Mahicanituck, who had the urge to explore its reaches to the south. They built canoes to travel on it and seek a home that would please their god. One after another, these tribes found their homes and settled down. The Weckquaeskecks built their village at what is now Dobbs Ferry and spread east to the Bronx River. But the Manhattes tribe continued on until they reached a place where the palisaded shores were high. They were puzzled by the river's flow, for at times the water moved upstream—the phenomenon of tides was new to them. Cautious but brave, they continued on, and finally landed by a small stream of clear fresh water. They had reached the island that was to be known as Manhattan.

Waters seemingly endless stretched to the south, and they felt far from their cousins. They re-entered their canoes, and now the tides urged them upstream. When they reached the mouth of a small stream where they had camped on their downriver journey, they turned again into this protected harbor. They named the stream Nepperhaem, and decided to build their first village there. They called it Nappeckamack in honor of the venerable sachem who had led them to their new home. Thus the first settlement on the site of what is now Yonkers was established.

In the course of time, the tribe became familiar with the great river and explored the two islands. They named the southern island Manahatin, and it became their favorite hunting and fishing ground.

As the Manhattes grew in numbers, a new sachem took over the two islands. He assumed the name Manatey in honor of his kingdom, and established his capital on the shores of the fresh-water lake, where he built a permanent village on the high western slope. From this hill he could see far across the East River to the lands beyond (Long Island), and far to the west across the Mahicanituck. The site of the village was covered with evergreen trees, large oaks and flowering shrubs. With the declining sun, the hill and trees cast intriguing shadows in the lake, and the waters reflected the changing colors of the skies. He called both village and lake Manahatta in honor of his beautiful Queen Manahattae, who in turn had been given this name because she reflected the glory of the enchanted isle.

The Great Spirit smiled upon the tribe, and moon after moon passed as the Manhattes grew and prospered. The rains pattered down pleasantly, and the lightning was inspiring to see. The thunder was the voice of their god speaking to them with satisfaction. They had found their paradise.

In time, bands of Manhattes moved across the Mahicanituck to its western shore (New Jersey), and developed into new sub-tribes, such as the Delawares. Other bands crossed the East River into the area now Brooklyn, becoming the Canarsies and other Long Island tribes, and still others migrated south to Staten Island.

Such is the legend of the beginning of Indian civilization on Manhattan Island and in the surrounding area. Part of this story is, of course, supposition, but most historians agree that the Manhattes were a part of the Mohican Nation, who descended the Mahicanituck, took possession of Manhattan Island, and owned it at the time Henry Hudson discovered it in 1609. All authorities seem to agree that the various tribes found in the vicinity of Manhattan spoke the Algonquin language; they must therefore either have migrated directly from the part of the West where this great Indian family lived, or have been an offshoot of one of its divisions as it expanded along the eastern coast.

The Indians, of course, had no written language, and it is not surprising that the early white settlers spelled Indian words in many different ways, such as Manhattes, Manahattes, Manahattans, Manahados, Manhattan and Manahatin. Juet, the mate on Hudson's ship, applied the name Manahatta to Manhattan, and also to the river on the island's western side. An English map of 1610 shows the name Manahatta for the New Jersey side and the name Manhatin for the island. On November 5, 1626, a Dutch official wrote that "they bought the Island of Manhattes from the wild men for the value of 60 guilders." [1] Vingboom's map of 1639 shows Manhattan Island under the name of Manatun. Historians refer to the Indian village (which they all agree was located on the shores of the great fresh-water lake) as Manahatta, Manahatin and Manados, and they all seem to use similar words for the name of

[1] The Dutch often referred to the Indians as the *Willden* or wild men.

the island: Minna-atn, Manahatin, Manatum and Manados. Callender, in *Yesterdays in Little Old New York*,[2] uses the name Manahatta for the village, and says that the village gave the island its name. He speaks of the Indian tribe as the Manhattes.

Since in the Indian era there were actually two islands, the Indians may for centuries have used two names, which would naturally have confused the Dutch. It should be remembered that the white race and the red were in actual contact on Manhattan for only a few years, and in the surrounding area for only about seventy-five in all—from 1624, when a few ships were arriving to trade, to around 1700; and it was very difficult for these two totally different civilizations to understand one another. But since each of these islands should, even now, have a recorded name, the northern one will hereafter be known as Manatun, and the one that lay to the south as Manhattan.

[2] James H. Callender, *Yesterdays in Little Old New York*. New York: Dorland Press, 1929.

CHAPTER III

The Indian Capital of Manahatta

The village of Manahatta was the first permanently inhabited place on Manhattan Island, and as such its site is today the island's historic center. Excavations for buildings in the vicinity have disclosed shell beds of immense size, denoting not only a large village, by Indian standards, but one long occupied.

By weaving together the legends that have come down, the topography of the land and accounts of the early Dutch settlers, it is possible to reconstruct a plausible plan of this village.

Like Manhattan Island, Manahatta Lake was actually not one lake but two. In the Dutch era these became known as Big Kolch and Little Kolch, and later, by popular usage, as Collect Pond. The two lakes covered an area now approximately bounded by the Bowery, Elm, Pearl, Lafayette and Canal Streets.

At the southern end of the large lake, where Big Kolch and Little Kolch joined, was a tiny point of land, called Kolchhoeck, meaning a point of land jutting into water. Worth Street today follows the point of land as the street crosses the old lake bed. The old Tombs Prison was built on solid land which had been an island in the larger lake. Even today the area formerly covered by Collect Pond is distinctly outlined, since it is lower than the surrounding area. This can be noticed if one stands at the southwest corner of Worth and Lafayette Streets, where once Kolchhoeck jutted out into the water.

The village of Manahatta was built on the elevation which now lies between Lafayette and Church Streets and White and Duane Streets. As the village expanded, some of the wigwams

9

and longhouses were built in the forest surrounding this area, but the heart and center of the capital was near the present intersection of Broadway and Worth Street. Instead of the square now formed by the street intersection, the trail-crossing in those days was a large circle used by the Indians for their outdoor gatherings—"Manahatta Circle."

This Circle was atop Manahatta Hill—the highest point on the southern island. Even though cut down by twenty-five feet when Broadway was extended, it is still one of the highest elevations between Canal Street and the Battery. The wigwam of the Grand Sachem, known as the Sackama Wicker, was built just southwest of Manahatta Circle. On the southeast was located the Indian treasury or money factory, where wampum was made from the shells collected on the East River shore and from the more distant parts of Long Island. On the northeast corner of this trail junction, between the present Catherine Lane and Worth Street, was a jagged promontory about seventy-five feet high, thrusting itself above the larger lake. This was the eastern portion of the hill later known as Kolch or Calch Hill. On this rugged promontory, probably two hundred feet square, the Manhattes built a fort or stockade. From Manahatta Circle trails led in every direction: the Kapsee Trail south, the Wampum Trail southeast, the Rechtanck Trail east, the Sappokanican Trail north and the Lapinikan Trail west.

The setting of the village was surprisingly strategic. It was the center of a self-sufficient area that afforded ample fresh water and plenty of food in either peace or war. At the northern edge of the village, near what is now the intersection of Canal Street and Broadway, the fort protected it against enemy canoes arriving through the water passage. An outer circle of defense was provided by Lapinikan Village on the Hudson, by Rechtanck on the East River, and Kapsee Village to the south. Manahatta Village itself was surrounded on three sides by an almost impenetrable swamp, which on the west lay along what is now West Broadway, on the north along Canal

Street, and on the east along what are now the Bowery and Roosevelt Street. The village snuggled securely in this horseshoe, the open end of which, facing south, had the strong natural protection of rock ridges.

Secure in this location, the Manhattes deserted the wigwams of the nomads and constructed permanent dwellings, some of which were rather large—one hundred feet long and fifteen to twenty feet wide. About ten families, each of which had its own "fireplace" and household utensils, were housed to a building. To construct these longhouses, hickory saplings were driven into the ground and the tops bent over and lashed together. Limbs and twigs were interlaced to form a frame, and dried cornstalks were woven horizontally to form walls and a roof, which, in turn, were covered by strips of bark laid on like shingles. Small openings were left at the top so that the smoke of each fireplace could escape, and a larger opening, just high enough to crawl through, was made in a side wall near the floor to serve as a doorway.

Each person had his own fur rug, and members of a family slept in a circle with their feet toward the fire built in the center of their allotted portion of the long room. Since wood was plentiful, the fires were kept burning continuously in cold weather because of the difficulty of rekindling them.

Some families who preferred individual homes went on living in wigwams, which were constructed in much the same way as longhouses except that they were small and round, with pointed tops. Thus it is seen that these earliest Manhattan-dwellers set the style still followed today: some lived in one-family houses, and others in large apartment houses!

Chapter IV

Life in the Village of Manahatta

Some of the early records of the explorers give an interesting account of Manhattan's citizens before contact with the white race changed many of their habits and customs.

The men were lithe and strong, with broad shoulders and narrow waists. Trained from youth to endure hardship, they could travel fast and carry heavy loads. The Manhattes braves ground out with stones or plucked with clamshells such hair as appeared on their sparsely bearded faces; they feared an old legend which said that those who grew hair on their faces would come back to earth after death in the form of an animal. Their attire was a double apron made of skins. For ceremonial affairs most of the braves had special aprons, sometimes brightly colored and beautifully beaded. Unlike the plains Indians, they wore no headdresses, but the hair was elaborately trimmed to form a cockscomb on top, about three inches wide and extending from the forehead over and down the back. For this trimming operation, too, sharp stones were used. It is difficult to reconcile the various drawings which show feathers adorning their hair, and in some instances even feathered headdresses, with descriptions of the Manhattes left by the first white settlers, who actually saw them. Apparently the early artists worked not from these authentic descriptions but from stories and pictures of red men of the West.

It is not too difficult to reconstruct daily life in the village of Manahatta. The routine was probably little different from that of other important Indian villages, except that in a capital there was a certain element of glamour and even mystery, as runners arrived from afar and chieftains made an impressive entrance with their retinues.

Fish was plentiful, and there was an abundance of wild game—rabbit, opossum, deer and bear. *Tuckah,* a large root or wild potato, grew abundantly in the lowlands and had good food value. The land was so fertile that farming was simplicity itself. Maize, pumpkins, melons and squash were among the principal crops. In winter, maize, or corn, was the staple diet. When prepared as porridge it was called *sapsis,* and when moistened and cooked on hot stones, *noohik.* To the white settlers, who could not properly accent the Indian word, noohik soon became known as nocake or hoecake. Tobacco was grown extensively, to be smoked by both men and women, and it seems evident that cotton, or some other form of fiber, was also grown, since some clothing and plaited fishing lines were made from fiber.

The size of the population of Manahatta probably varied according to the food supply. Grain was planted as far south as the present City Hall Park and in the fertile area east of the lake described in 1651 as the "Land Called Werpoes," but few Manhattes wished to leave the magic shores of the lake.

The Sackama Wicker, the wigwam of the Grand Sachem, was the first news center on Manhattan Island—the clearinghouse for word brought by travelers and messengers using the trails centering in the capital village. News traveled farther and more rapidly than might be thought possible under these primitive conditions. Signal fires on the high hill could be seen for miles in all directions, and smoke signals were sent with ease from this first "broadcasting station." Visitors were housed in a beautiful wooded section northwest of Manahatta Circle, in the area now bounded by Worth, Leonard, Broadway and Church Streets. These "wigwamtels" were Manhattan's first hotels. And the forerunner of every "P.S." in Manhattan was the longhouse school, situated on the south side of the present Worth Street between Broadway and Church

Street, where the children sat in rapt attention as one of their elders recited the legends of the past.

Each family in the village made its own tools and equipment. These, in general, consisted of several sharp-pointed sticks and stones for farming, bows and arrows for hunting, spears, a kind of fishhook, and at least one canoe. The canoes were not the light birchbark creations of some Indian tribes, but blunt-nosed boats made laboriously, though expertly, by hollowing out heavy logs with controlled fire.

Today the three blocks of Worth Street from Lafayette to West Broadway, and the five blocks from White to Duane Streets, mark the site of the ancient Indian capital. As to when this early Indian village was established, there is no certainty. But, from legends and present-day research, it is probable that the red men arrived in New York State about four thousand years ago, and reasonable to assume that they were not too many generations in finding the outlet to the great river. The village may have been in existence three thousand years ago. This year (1953) Rome is celebrating its 2705th anniversary and Paris its 2000th, both of these historic cities basing their founding dates on legend. Manahatta may well be older than either one of these.

Accordingly, Worth Street should this year celebrate not only its one hundredth anniversary as a textile center but also the three hundredth anniversary of the incorporation of the city, the 344th anniversary of Hudson's discovery of Manahatin, and the 3000th anniversary as the first inhabited spot on Manhattan Island.

The City of New York could well join with Worth Street to make this celebration a city-wide affair. It could be built around a great water pageant on the Hudson, "The Discoverers Come to Town." This could begin with a colorful flotilla of two thousand canoes, manned by members of the various canoe clubs dressed in Indian costume, descending the Hudson to land on the shore and parade to the old site of the Indian village in Worth Street. Next, Henry Hudson could sail up the bay in the *Half-Moon* and then into the Hudson, followed by two thousand sailboats with flags flying. He could land on the shore and discover the Indians again. A great celebration and a big powwow could follow. Manhattan Island would offer a great background to the river setting, and the navy and ship lines could add glamour to the surroundings. It could be a spectacle worthy of New York.

CHAPTER V

The Dutch Come

September 14, 1609, is a memorable day in the history of the world and in the annals of Worth Village. On that day Indian fishermen on the shores of the Mahicanituck reported a "great white bird" floating up the river, guided by strange men with white skins.

Henry Hudson, in his ship the *Half-Moon*—an eighty-ton vessel about fifty-eight feet long and sixteen feet wide, manned by a crew of twenty—had sailed from New Amsterdam on April 4, 1609, seeking the fabled Northwest Passage to India. More than five months later he entered the river which was afterward to bear his name. Dropping anchor, Hudson went ashore in a small boat, and with members of his crew was received in a friendly fashion by the Indians.

History does not record the exact spot where he landed, but an analysis of the known facts enables us to identify it with reasonable accuracy. In this period there were three Indian settlements along the river. The first was Kapsee, a small outpost at the very toe of the southern island. The next was Lapinikan, where the stream of the same name entered the river at a point now marked by Canal Street. And then came Sappokanican, a half-mile farther north, at the mouth of Minetta Brook. Hudson was most anxious to find a passage to Asia, and it is plausible to believe that once he saw a long straight body of water he would land to question the natives. It does not seem reasonable that he would have landed at Kapsee, for from that point he could not see up the river and could not tell whether it was a bay or a passage. But when he

16

reached a point off Lapinikan he could see up the river for a
great distance, and there was then no reason to go farther.

We may therefore assume that Hudson landed at the village
of Lapinikan, which was the river port of the Indian capital
of Manahatta. (An early drawing showing this landing is reproduced in the pictorial section of this book.) The actual site
of Lapinikan was near the present village of Worth, a matter
of what today would be five or six city blocks. At that time
the shore line of the Hudson had not yet been filled in, as may
be seen from early maps of the island.

One legend gives an amusing account of the now historic
welcoming ceremony:

> When Henry Hudson, and his crew, the first white
> men to set foot on the island, landed, they found the In-
> dians peaceful though skeptical and reserved, waiting to
> see whether the strangers were friend or foe. Desiring to
> be friendly and as a peaceful gesture, the white men of-
> fered the Indians a drink of rum. Not knowing what it
> was and fearing to trust the strangers too far, the Indians
> hesitated to accept it. The white men showed their dis-
> appointment, feeling that it reflected doubt upon their
> good intentions. After a tense moment or two, the Indian
> Sachem of Manahatta quietly stepped forward. He re-
> minded his braves that it was a custom of their race to be
> courteous to visitors and smoke the Pipe of Peace with
> friends. He then took another step forward and, in a
> voice which all could hear, firmly said, "If these are
> friends, the drink offering will not harm me, and if they
> are enemies, I am ready to sacrifice myself to uphold the
> honor and tradition of our tribe." With some apprehen-
> sion, the Sachem accepted the container, raised it in his
> hand with a friendly gesture to the visitors and his tribe,
> and then took a long drought. As the firewater burned
> down to his toes, he thought his end had come and that
> the visitors had tricked him into drinking liquid fire. It
> required iron nerve to control himself so he could retain
> his dignity and die like a great Sachem without fear.
> Expecting the end at any moment, he quietly folded
> his arms, and, looking his visitors straight in the eyes,

put up an heroic front. He knew that his braves would
avenge not only his death but the insult to the tribe. He
would show these strangers, however, that a Sachem was
without fear.

In a few moments, however, one foot trembled
slightly, the other shifted easily and a finger twitched. His
retinue, watching closely, thought the beginning of the
end had come and uneasy frowns appeared on their faces.
Shortly, a wee smile lighted the old Sachem's face, which
amazed his warriors, for in the past he had seldom
smiled. Again his feet shifted easily, he slowly unfolded
his arms and quietly rubbed his hands together. He began to look pleased, more animated and more friendly.
Then, without further warning, he walked up to Henry
Hudson, raised his hand aloft, Indian fashion, in a
friendly How! How! . . . He welcomed them to his Island
Kingdom and to Manahatta, his capital village. Then
turning to his assembled braves, he urged them to have a
drink of the friendly water and to prepare a feast for his
friends.

And so to the long list of "firsts" in the history of Worth
Street may be added the first "Manhattan"—the firewater kind,
that is.

How cordial was Hudson's actual welcome can only be sur-
mised. But we do know that, believing he had discovered the
Northwest Passage, he was eager to be on his way. Soon the
Half-Moon's anchor was raised, and the ship proceeded up
the great river.

The strange ship and its strange crew naturally caused a
great amount of interest and excitement among the Indians.
Whether a bird or a canoe, it was much larger than anything
they had seen before. Many paddled out in their canoes for a
closer view. Two Indians, bolder than the rest, climbed aboard.
The ship's crew detained them as curiosities.

As the *Half-Moon* proceeded up the river, it soon passed
the Indian village of Sappokanican (tobacco fields) at the
confluence of Minetta Brook, which stream had its origin near
what is now Greenwich Village.

It soon passed Nipinicksen, a fortified village on the mainland near the mouth of Spuyten Duyvil Creek (Harlem River) which was the stronghold for the capital village of Nappeckamack (Yonkers) about four miles farther north.

As the ship passed this point, the two Indians escaped. They began to arouse the Manhattes in that region against the strangers with stories of their mistreatment while aboard the vessel. These stories were evidently exaggerated, but feverish preparations were made to attack the ship should it return.

On October 2, 1609, after exploring the upper reaches of the river as far as Albany and finding no passage to the Indies, Hudson finally sailed down the river. The aroused Indians attacked the *Half-Moon* when it arrived off Spuyten Duyvil Creek.

In a furious and bloody battle the Indians suffered heavy losses. This was probably the first planned naval battle in the New World. But, more important, it marked the turning point in the affairs of the Indians, because here they suffered the first of many subsequent reverses at the hands of the white man.

After this encounter Hudson decided that it would be foolhardy for him to remain in the vicinity with his small crew. The Indians of Manahatta were relieved when they saw the *Half-Moon* begin its voyage toward the wide waters of the ocean. But his departure did not fully relieve their anxiety, for now they had lost the feeling of security in their island kingdom.

Henry Hudson was an Englishman, a brave man and an intrepid explorer. He had already sailed twice for the English Muscovy Company seeking the Northwest Passage, penetrating first to Spitzbergen and later to Novaya Zemlya (Nova Zembla) in the ship *Hopewell*.

On the voyage during which he explored the river that was to bear his name he was under the authority of the Dutch East India Company. Upon returning to Holland he reported his discovery to his employers, but these men had little interest in colonizing a new land; the lure of trade with the spice isles and silken East offered greater profit.

Hudson sailed once again, in an English ship, the *Discovery*, and found the great Canadian bay that bears his name. On this voyage his crew mutinied and on June 23, 1611, cast him, his son and six others adrift in a small boat. Hudson and his companions faded into the icy mists forever.

Other explorers had earlier located the famous river, but none of them had tried to enter or to claim it. Now the Dutch suddenly began to take notice of the New World. They named the river after the intrepid Englishman, and followed up his voyage with several others, notably that of Adriaen Block. On the strength of these various expeditions, they laid claim to Manhattan and the surrounding area.

CHAPTER VI

The First and Greatest Textile Transaction

In 1614, the Dutch decided to colonize the New World of which Hudson had spoken in glowing terms. But it was not until May 4, 1626, that settlers arrived under Peter Minuit. They landed on the southeastern tip of the island in order to avoid the village of Kapsee on the southwestern side. The Dutch, with memories of their homeland still fresh in their minds, preferred the lowlands, and soon began building houses and a fort, which Minuit named Fort Amsterdam.

The new settlers' homes were erected along the shore in haphazard fashion, each selecting his own site. In time paths were worn from house to house, from the group of houses to the water's edge, and to the spring near the Indian trail that is now Broadway. As the little settlement grew to a hundred homes, the paths became narrow roads that followed the same routes. Thus developed the irregular pattern of present-day streets in the congested area south of Wall Street and east of Broadway. For several years the northern limit of the little settlement was a heavy picket fence or palisaded wall erected as a barrier against the Indians. The narrow irregular road inside the wall became the famous Wall Street of today.

After many differences with the Indians and many pow-wows, Minuit, in November 1626, decided to buy the island from them. He dealt with the sachem of Manahatta. According to some historians the price paid was "beads and trinkets" to the value of sixty guilders, or about twenty-four dollars in today's money. There seem to be no factual records, however, to prove that "beads and trinkets" were the actual medium of exchange. As one studies this transaction, a feeling arises that the "beads and trinkets" tradition came about in an effort to show how cheaply the Island was bought from the Indians. It seems much more reasonable that the merchandise which attracted the Indians was fabric or cloth, which they saw the Europeans wearing and which was something novel to them and hence of great value.

These Indians made their own beads and trinkets, designed and fashioned from shell, bone and wood—and these were distinctive enough to attract the Europeans by their beauty. The Manhattes were highly skilled in making beads. For this reason alone it would seem doubtful that they could be persuaded to sell their island, lakeside village and their homes for articles which they already possessed and could make themselves.

On the other hand, they were greatly interested in textiles, which they did not possess and could not make, except possibly in very crude forms. They had seen Hudson's bright red coat and they were familiar with, and probably envious of, the clothes worn by the Dutch settlers.

If additional proof were needed to establish the bargaining power of textiles with the Indians, it would only be necessary to study the lists of items later traded for lands in what is now Westchester County. These authentic records list cloth, shirts, stockings and blankets, as well as knives, powder, axes and other useful items.

With these facts in mind, it is intriguing to find an old picture of the purchase of Manhattan in which the Dutch are shown displaying many yards of cloth before the Indians. An Indian maid is admiring and coveting a belt or sash made of fabric. This artist was far closer to the truth than the legend of "beads and trinkets."

In the original transaction the Indians were concerned mainly with the value of their capital village Manahatta and their lake with its fresh-water supply. The rest of the island was thrown in for good measure.

The sale of Manhattan was undoubtedly the greatest real estate transaction in the history of the world. The price paid for Manhattan's 22,000 acres in 1626 was about one-tenth of a cent per acre, whereas today the same ground is valued at a million dollars an acre.

CHAPTER VII

An Historic Murder in Manahatta

In 1626, the year of the purchase, an act was committed which was to cause terrible consequences for the colony in later years but which, on the other hand, eventually was to prove a milestone in the progress of the world toward democratic government.

A Weckquaeskeck Indian from Keskeskeck (Westchester County) with his young nephew set out from his home with beaver skins to trade with the Dutch. As they were passing along the trail in the vicinity of the village of Manahatta, they met three farm servants in the employ of Director-General Minuit. These three killed the elder Indian and seized the furs. The boy escaped and returned to his people with the story of the murder. And although some years passed before the next episode, the boy never forgot.

Meanwhile, Dutch relations with the Indians became more and more strained, and many difficulties developed. Director-General Kieft, who had succeeded Minuit, was an autocrat with sole authority from the Dutch West India Company to rule the colony as he saw fit. His decision to levy tribute on the Indians to raise money for the support of the colony, and his general carelessness in dealing with them, contributed to the unrest.

Suddenly the island was stirred by momentous news. Claes Smit, a wheelwright, had been murdered by the same Weckquaeskeck Indian who, as a boy, had seen his uncle killed and plundered. This Indian arrived by canoe at the small store operated by Smit near what is now Forty-fifth Street and the

24

East River. He asked to see some cloth, and while the store-keeper's back was turned the Indian killed Smit and then fled to the safety of his home in Aquehung, a village in Keskeskeck, now Yonkers.

By a fantastic coincidence, the spot where Claes Smit was killed—the first "international incident" in Manhattan—is the present site of the United Nations Headquarters. Here a man was killed to avenge an earlier murder about which he knew nothing. The avenging act was carried out legally under the code of the Indian nation, but nevertheless was in direct conflict with the laws of the Dutch. A problem of international law was posed which would echo down the years.

Director-General Kieft demanded satisfaction and the surrender of the killer, which the Weckquaeskecks refused. At odds with the Indians in general, the Director was anxious to make war to exterminate them. The Dutch, however, had been uneasy for some time about Kieft, and it was even hinted that he desired war with the Indians so that he might minimize his mismanagement of the colony. For this reason he did not dare take full responsibility for a war to punish the murderer of Smit, so he called together a committee made up of the heads of the twelve leading families of New Amsterdam. This was the first time in the history of the colony that the people were consulted on a public question, hence the meeting has become historic as the first move toward democratic government in Manhattan.

Actually, Kieft planned to use the committee as a front. He laid before them several questions worded in such a way that, if answered, they would give him authority to start a war. The committee, however, objected to the form of the questions, and the matter was left unsettled for the time being.

Nevertheless, in the winter of 1641 he moved against the Indians in what is now Westchester. The small military force returned without any action, having been completely outmaneuvered by the Indians. A compromise was reached in which the tribe agreed to turn over the killer. But the Indian had become a hero to his fellows, and the Dutch were never able to enforce the agreement.

The year 1643 turned out to be a bloody one. Small raids and massacres marked the early stages of the war. Finally, eleven Algonquin tribes joined together against the Dutch, and a furious war of revenge ensued. Within a week's time the Indians destroyed most of the homes and farms in Long Island, lower Westchester and practically all of Manhattan outside the Fort on the lower tip. Calch Hook Farm, now Worth Village, was completely overrun. This serious blow to the colony might have marked the end of it if the Indians had followed up their advantage.

The committee of twelve sent an appeal for help to Holland, but help from that source was slow in arriving. While they vainly waited, John Underhill and a force of English settlers from Long Island surprised several Indian villages there, killing and capturing many of the warriors. They then took the offensive on the mainland in Westchester County, where they defeated the Indians in a great battle near the present site of Port Chester in which approximately seven hundred were killed or captured. This broke the spirit of the red men, and ended the Indian wars for several years.

The exact spot on Manhattan where the first Indian was killed and plundered has never been stated. History does not even record his name. But historians say that he was traveling along the Indian trail on Manhattan Island carrying furs for sale at Fort Amsterdam, and that he was killed on the old trail at a spot near, or in the vicinity of, Collect Pond.

The location of the lake is well known, and so are the locations of the old trails. One trail led from the Indian village of Rechtanck (Corlear's Hook) on the East River, along the general line of what is now East Broadway, to Chatham Square; across what is now Worth Street, and thence to the east of Collect Pond, along what is now Park Row, to a junction. From here, one branch led south to join the Kapsee

Trail below what is now City Hall. The other branch followed the general line of what is now Pearl Street and followed the south bank of Collect Pond to join the Kapsee Trail (now Broadway) at the village of Manahatta.

The fact that the Indian was carrying his furs overland raises the question whether or not his destination was really Fort Amsterdam. The Dutch had undoubtedly established a trading post at the southern edge of the Indian village of Manahatta, on the old Kapsee Trail (now Broadway), where daily bargains were made. This Indian was very likely headed for that post. A Weckquaeskeck Indian from distant Keskeskeck would hardly leave his canoe at Rechtanck Village after traveling down the Harlem and East Rivers by water and then proceed afoot for two miles or more to Fort Amsterdam, carrying his heavy load of furs. Had he been going to the latter place, he could have more easily completed his journey by canoe.

Granting these suppositions, it would seem that the historic spot where Manhattan's first murder occurred was probably the corner of Duane Street and Broadway.

CHAPTER VIII

The Indians Leave Manahatta

The Dutch ruled Manhattan Island for about forty years. In general it was a period of turmoil and unrest, with continual differences with the Indians; it must be remembered that the Dutch were forcing their way in, taking Indian lands with only token payments, and attempting to outbargain the Indians for their furs. The Dutch made no particular attempt to placate the Indians, placing their entire reliance on force.

For twenty years after its founding, the settlement of New Amsterdam made little progress, and the venture seemed doomed to failure. According to old records, the settlers became so lonely and so homesick that they gathered day after day at the toe of the island, and many tears were shed when no ships arrived to encourage them. That point of land became known as Weeper's Point.

Ten years after their arrival, the Dutch began to bring in slaves for heavy work. The rugged terrain, and the presence of so many rocks, tree stumps and roots, made farming difficult until the ground could be prepared. But despite all the discouragements, there was a destiny for this island that could not be ignored, and the Dutch pioneers had their traditional trait of persistence.

After the Dutch took control, Manahatta Village soon lost its importance. The governing center of the island became Fort Amsterdam, and the lake and the area around it reverted to a fishing place and hunting ground. By 1636 the Indians had completely abandoned their capital village, the present

28

site of the Village of Worth, and Jan Jansen Damen moved
in. So thoroughly did Damen establish himself that on April
19, 1638, the Dutch West Indies Company leased him two
large plots of ground. The enterprise of Damen is all the more
remarkable when one realizes that in 1639 there were only
thirty small farms on the entire island.

The Dutch pioneer named the site Calk Hook Farm. Calk,
sometimes spelled Calck, appears to be a corruption of the
Dutch word *calch,* meaning a small body of water. Calk Hook
came from Kalchhoek, which meant "Lime Corner." There
are also old references to Kalch Hill or Kolch Hill, and to
Kolchhoeck, a peninsula jutting into the Kalch or Kolch Pond.
(As earlier noted, this hook or point of land jutted into Manahatta Lake from the west, from where Worth Street now inter-
sects Lafayette Street, and was part of the barrier which
divided the two lakes.) The Dutch first gave the name of Calch
to the lake the Indians called Manahatta, but in time that
name was corrupted to Kalch or Kolch, and the two lakes
became Big Kolch and Little Kolch. Later, by common usage,
the water area became Collect Pond.

Damen named his farm for the hill and the hook which
were part of it. After ten years of labor he finally applied for
ownership of the land, and Director-General Kieft conveyed
it to him on March 16, 1646. According to the records, the
farm contained "20 morgens, three hundred eighty-six yards,"
or about fifty acres. The farm was at that time considered far
north of the Dutch settlement of New Amsterdam. It extended
from a line on the south, approximately the present Reade
Street, to the edge of the swamp on the north, near Canal
Street. Then it ran from the shores of the lakes on the east,
the present Lafayette Street, to the edge of the swamp on the
west, roughly a line about halfway between Church Street and
West Broadway. At some time prior to October 17, 1661,
after Damen died, the farm was divided into four nearly equal
parts by his heirs. Roughly, the dividing lines followed what
is now Broadway as a north and south line, and Leonard

Street as an east and west line. The history of this farm is told at greater length in Chapter XI.

While Damen was struggling to establish his farm, the little settlement of New Amsterdam was also struggling to establish itself. The sale of firearms and powder to the Indians was prohibited. Later the Indians were ordered to pay tribute in furs, which act finally led to an uprising. As a result, the first militia company was formed for mutual protection, every man capable of bearing arms being enrolled.

Despite all his difficulties, Peter Minuit, while Director-General of the colony, had authorized two shipbuilders to construct a vessel which was to be one of the largest then afloat. The Dutch had discovered that the tall evergreen trees growing on Manhattan Island and the mainland of West-chester were suitable for masts taller than any known. This would permit the construction of larger ships. An eight-hundred-ton ship, ten times as large as the *Half-Moon* and named the *New Netherlands,* was finally built, and used to publicize the new colony. So successful was this vessel that its building opened up an era of larger ships.

The Dutch set up a school for their children as early as 1633. It had about twenty pupils, who received the rudiments of an education in a small one-room cabin which was also used as the village hall.

There was a great change for the better in the fortunes of the Dutch colony when Peter Stuyvesant succeeded to the governorship in 1647. He took the first steps to placate the Indians. The village of New Amsterdam took on new life as the fort was rebuilt, a council formed, new streets laid out and public order restored. The social status of the community was raised considerably by the arrival of Mrs. Stuyvesant and her sister, who were prominent Dutch ladies.

So rapid was the progress of the settlement under Stuyvesant that on February 2, 1653, the growing village of New Amsterdam was incorporated and the present City of New York had its formal beginning.

In the earliest days the costumes of the settlers were simple and durable, in general made for wear rather than appearances. After the arrival of Stuyvesant and his lady, and as the wealth of individuals increased, the men and women began to dress more carefully.

Some of the early records disclose that the women, to be properly dressed, wore several petticoats of different colors at the same time. Lace and aprons were seen everywhere. The men were in style when wearing several pairs of breeches at the same time, along with their square-cut coats and fancy waistcoats trimmed with lace and ruffles.

The Dutch era added great fame to the historic Indian village of Manahatta, for the sale of this village and both islands to the Dutch marked the beginning of the modern Manhattan. The island was now destined for a great future in an ever-expanding new world.

CHAPTER IX

The English Come

Events were taking place abroad in the early 1660's that were to affect the history of Manhattan. The Stuart kings had been restored in England, and war was declared on Holland. In 1664 King Charles granted his brother, the Duke of York, all the land extending from the Connecticut River to Delaware Bay, including Manhattan. An English squadron arrived off New Amsterdam on August 18, 1664, and blockaded the port. On September 8th the Dutch surrendered, and New Amsterdam became an English colony.

A map dated 1664, shown later, entitled "The Duke's Plan for the Towne of Mannados or New Amsterdam," lays out a plan for the village. Some of the old street names are interesting. The village was referred to as Mannados, one of the several spellings for the Indian village of Manahatta. Soon, however, the name was changed to New York.

The British immediately set about reorganizing the colony. Colonel Richard Nicolls became the new governor, and proved an excellent choice. He established a new council and the English form of municipal government, consisting of a mayor, sheriff and aldermen, a form which has persisted to this day.

New York now came under the English flag for a period that was to last, save for a brief interval, until the American Revolution. In 1672, while the Dutch and English were still at war, a Dutch fleet appeared off Manhattan. The settlement surrendered and briefly became New Orange in honor of the Prince of Orange. At the end of the year peace was declared,

32

and Manhattan was returned to the English and again became New York.

To prevent difficulties with the inhabitants and to secure their cooperation in developing New York, the English in 1686 issued the Dongan Charter, which confirmed the early patents of the Dutch government to land on Manhattan Island. From a real estate point of view this action was most important. Furthermore, all these briefs and patents have been found. The first recorded land conveyance in the Worth Street area by the Dutch—subsequently confirmed by the English—was, as we have seen, the conveyance of Kalchhoeck to Jan Jansen Damen, dated March 16, 1646.

About this time Frederick Philipse became a man of great importance and influence, and he may be regarded as New York's first great merchant prince. The story of his rise to wealth and influence from humble beginnings is one that was often to be repeated in the annals of Manhattan.

Frederick Philipse was active in New Amsterdam as a carpenter, architect, builder and dealer in real estate. Later his genius as a trader established him as the leading merchant of the New World. Lands and mills, together with foreign commerce, river traffic and Indian trade, contributed to his wealth. In 1662 he married Margaret Hardenbrook, a woman who possessed both beauty and business acumen. She aided her husband greatly and had a part in the establishment of the great manor at Yonkers. She also bought and sold on her own account, operated ships and frequently went to Holland to attend to commercial matters. Margaret Hardenbrook Philipse may well be looked upon as New York's first businesswoman. She died in 1691, and a year later Frederick Philipse married Catherine Van Cortlandt, who was young and comely. It was this second wife who enjoyed the honor of being made Lady Philipse when William and Mary, by Royal Charter dated June 12, 1693, changed Philipse's possessions into the Lordship or Manor of Philipsborough. Frederick Philipse died at the height of his glory in 1702.

He was undoubtedly the first great textile merchant in Manhattan. In addition to trading and selling merchandise, he loaned money, taking all sorts of articles as security. For example, in 1664 one Anneke Ryzen brought suit against him for the return of her gown and petticoats, which she had pledged with him in return for a loan of 160 guilders.

This was one of the earliest lawsuits in Manhattan of which we have a record—if not the first; and it was about petticoats.

CHAPTER X

The First Hundred Years in Old New York

By 1709, a hundred years after Hudson's discovery, the population of Manhattan Island was about four thousand, most of whom still lived south of Wall Street, near the tip of the Island.

But beginnings were being made toward building a metropolis. As early as 1670 a commission was set up to pave the streets as evenly as possible. Each street had a single gutter running down the middle. Stone Street was the first to be paved; ballast stones from incoming ships were used for the purpose.

In 1683 the little city was divided into six wards, which included the land from the Battery to Canal Street. The Worth Street area was in the Sixth Ward. A seventh ward was set up to include all land on the island north of what is now Canal Street. This meant that the lower island had six wards and the upper island only one.

An attempt at street lighting was made in 1697, when it was ordered that from December to March, during periods of moonless nights, every seventh house was to hang out a lantern.

There were also fire prevention laws. In 1648 the authorities issued an order that no more wooden or clay plaited chimneys were to be erected between the "fort and fresh water." This meant that the Worth Street area was even then regarded as part of the "city." Fines for violating the order were to be used for the purchase of ladders and leather fire buckets.

By 1664 the fire hazards were causing great concern. More and more lightly constructed houses were being jammed into

35

a limited area, and the fire fighting equipment consisted only
of leather buckets of water passed along from man to man.
So serious did all this become that in 1687 every resident who
had a house with two chimneys was required to supply one
fire bucket, and for more than two hearths two buckets were
required. Bakers had to keep three buckets in their shops, and
brewers six. Everyone who had a bucket was under orders to
report to every fire.

In due time the council decided that the village was expanding into a town, so a law was passed to prevent the shooting
of partridge and game in the streets.

The authorities issued an edict with reference to Collect
Pond, which at the time was far to the north. The wording of
this order shows the legal detail employed in those early days
to make even a fishing regulation effective.

> If any person hereafter presume to put, place or cast
> into the pond commonly called Fresh Water pond be-
> longing to this corporation any hoop net, draw net, purse
> net, casting net, cod net, bley net, or any other net or
> nets whatsoever, and shall take and catch any of the fish
> within the said pond therein or by any other engine,
> machine, arts, ways or means whatsoever other than by
> angling with angle rod, hook and line only, he shall pay
> a fine of forty shillings.

There were "traffic" problems, but far different from those
of today. Complaint was made to the Town Council that hogs
running loose to root in the streets kept the highways in dis-
repair. An ordinance was issued forthwith that permitted anyone to kill a hog running loose in the streets. This offered no
solution, since neighbors hesitated to kill each other's hogs.
Then followed days of furious debate. The Council finally
passed an ordinance directing the owner of each hog to put
an iron ring through its nose to prevent rooting.

On the land in what is now the Worth Street section were
many orchards, where peaches, apples and other fruit grew

abundantly, along with wild berries and nuts. It requires little imagination to picture a spring day in Worth Village in about 1700, with a flowering landscape interspersed with evergreens from Broadway down the long hill to the Hudson!

CHAPTER XI

The Rutgers Farm

Nowhere else in the world does there seem to be so much history involved in the titles to various parcels of real estate as in Manhattan. A comprehensive history of the great City of New York might be written from these records alone.

The first recorded land conveyance in the Worth Street area took place on March 16, 1646, when Kalchhoeck Farm was conveyed to Jan Jansen Damen. Chapter VIII contains the details of this transaction. After Damen's death, the farm was divided into four nearly equal parts.

Abram Verplanck bought the southwest quarter (Lot No. 1). His heirs sold it on February 27, 1697, to William Huddestone, who in turn sold it to Captain Richard Hill on March 24, 1702. Captain Hill sold the plot to Anthony Rutgers on February 4, 1723.

The northwest quarter (Lot No. 3) was sold to Augusters Heermans on October 17, 1661. Heermans sold it to Petrus Stuyvesant on a date not now known. Stuyvesant in turn sold it to Thomas Lewis, whose heirs sold it to Anthony Rutgers in November 1725.

The northeast quarter (Lot No. 4) came into the possession of Isaac Bedlow, but no deed seems to have been recorded showing the transaction. However, Bedlow died in 1673, and his heirs sold their interest to Jacobus van Cortlandt, who in turn sold it to Anthony Rutgers in 1725.

The remainder of the Damen farm (Lot No. 2), the southeast quarter, was sold to Jan Vigne. On March 30, 1708, Peter Roos, his heir, conveyed the plot to Jacques Fountain, who promptly sold it to Wolfert Webber. Webber sold it to Anthony Rutgers in 1725.

Thus Anthony Rutgers in the course of two years, from 1723 to 1725, acquired the entire Calk Hook Farm, located on the site of the Indian village of Manahatta.

The same Anthony Rutgers had in 1717 purchased a tract of land lying northwest of the intersection of what is now Chambers Street and Broadway—the strip between Chambers and Reade Streets, extending westward to the Hudson River and including the area between the swamp along West Broadway and the Hudson River as far north as the swamp along the creek now Canal Street. This North River Farm of about sixty-five acres was originally the Roe Loff Jansen Farm in 1636, the Bogardus Bowerie in 1638, and later part of the Duke's Farm.

By his purchases between 1717 and 1725, Anthony Rutgers became the owner of all the land between what is now Chambers, Lafayette and Canal Streets and the Hudson River. It appears that these purchases gave him title to the ponds or lakes, Big Kolch and Little Kolch, but for some reason not to the adjoining swampland, probably because they were earlier considered worthless and he had made no claim to them.

In 1730, however, he presented a petition to the authorities in England for a grant of these swamplands so that he might drain the area and, incidentally, secure more fertile land to pay for the drainage costs. (Rutgers suffered severely from malaria and wished to drain the swamps, which he shrewdly suspected were the cause.) The lower level of the land along West Broadway and Canal Street is a reminder of Anthony Rutgers' mosquito-infested swamp, for when they were later filled in after draining the level was not brought up to that of the surrounding area.

Rutgers' petition was granted on August 12, 1731. At that time he was living on Smith Street, now William Street, and was popularly known as Captain Rutgers. He had owned the Smith Street house since 1705. Having now organized a great estate, sometimes referred to as "Rutgers' North River Estate" but more often as "Rutgers' Farm," in about the year 1730 he built a fine mansion on a plot that faced the old Kapsee Trail (Broadway) at Duane Street.

Anthony Rutgers' grandfather was Rutger Jacobsen van Schoenderwoerdt, a man of considerable repute, who left Holland to settle at Fort Orange, or Albany, in 1636. Anthony's father was Harmon Rutgers, who moved to New Amsterdam from Albany in 1639 when the Indians in that area were causing trouble. Anthony first married Hendrickje Vandewater of New York, and after her death he married a widow named Cornelia Benson. He was an alderman of the City of New York from 1727 to 1734, and a member of the Colonial Assembly from 1726 to 1737.

The original Anthony Rutgers, who for convenience will be called Anthony I, died in 1746 leaving two sons, Peter and Anthony II, and five daughters. Both Peter and Anthony II had sons whom they named Anthony. Peter's son Anthony, a lawyer, married Elizabeth Williams; two years after he died, in 1754, she married Colonel Frederick Philipse, the third Lord of Philipse Manor.

Peter's sister Elsie, the daughter of Anthony I, married Leonard Lispenard in 1741. In 1748 Lispenard bought the other shares and took over the Rutgers Farm, which soon became known as Lispenard Farm. He completed the plan for draining the swamps and turned them into farm land, which, around what is now Canal Street, became known as Lispenard's Meadows.

Anthony III, son of Anthony II, became owner of the old family mansion and a portion of the land in the southwest quarter. The famous mansion finally, around 1760, became Ranelagh or Ranleigh Gardens, a place of amusement where food and drink were served and a band played on Mondays and Thursdays. It was very popular with those who wished to drive out into what was then the country. This place should not, however, be confused with the lesser known but still popular tavern known during the Revolution as the Ranleigh House. Properly titled the White Conduit House, it was located between what is now Worth and Leonard Streets on Broadway.

CHAPTER XII

Colonial New York

By 1765 the population of Manhattan had grown to 12,000, and the northern line of the city had moved to Chambers Street. It took almost a hundred and forty years, 1626 to 1765, for the Dutch and English settlement to expand northward one mile from the Battery. Four years later, in 1769, the city's population had leaped to 20,000, and the entire Crown Colony numbered 300,000. The city's population was still mostly below Cortlandt Street, although Broadway had inched its way as far as Vesey Street. The wealthy lived in Maiden Lane and State Street.

In the 1760's the people of New York had begun to join those of the other colonies in protests against the acts of George III. There was excitement everywhere, and resistance was becoming more and more pronounced. The Patriots Society was started in 1760 to oppose British tyranny. Secret societies were formed to oppose Crown officers attempting to collect taxes and levies.

Despite all this unrest, plans were made and carried out for the establishment of a hospital, a truly philanthropic institution. The first incorporated hospital in America, the Pennsylvania Hospital, had already been established by Benjamin Franklin in Philadelphia, in 1751. The first hospital in New York had its beginning at King's College, now Columbia University, where a medical department was installed in 1767. At the first graduation exercises, March 16, 1769, two medical students received their degrees. Dr. Samuel Bard, of the medical college faculty, made an earnest plea before a notable assembly for the establishment in New York of "a hospital for the sick poor of the colony, which would serve as a medical school."

The Hospital Association was organized in 1770. On June 13, 1771, through the efforts of the Earl of Dunmore, a Royal Charter was issued by King George III to the "Society of the Hospital of New York in America." The Colonial Assembly then approved an annual appropriation of £800 for twenty years. On June 23, 1772, Anthony and Gerthrude Rutgers sold, for 2,000 English pounds, to the above-mentioned Society, a plot of ground bounded as follows: 327 feet on Anthony Street—now Worth Street; 440 feet on Church Street; 338 feet on Hospital Street—now Duane Street; 440 feet on Broadway. This included the area between what is now Broadway and Worth, Duane and Church Streets. These five acres were about half of the southwest quarter of the old Damen or Calk Hook Farm. The Merchants Club, the Springs Building, the 40 Worth Street Building, the Cone Building, the Milliken Building and the buildings between Worth and Leonard Streets west of Broadway are all on this plot.

The cornerstone of the hospital was laid by Governor Tryon on September 3, 1773. Unfortunately, on February 28, 1775, when the main structure was just about completed, a fire occurred which consumed the interior of the building. The workmen were at dinner at the time and the suggested cause was that "shavings were too near a fire."

An appeal for funds was made, with the result that the Colonial Assembly authorized 4,000 English pounds for reconstruction. But by the time this work was begun the Revolutionary War had started. The New York Committee of Safety ordered the building prepared to house Colonial troops. Breastworks were thrown up about the building, and troops were posted to protect the city. Several wounded patriots were received in this building on July 12, 1776. These men were injured in an engagement when two British warships forced a passage up the Hudson. It is said that a cannonball from one of these landed on the hospital grounds. With the capture of the city by the British in September 1776, control of the building passed to British and Hessian troops, who used it as a barracks and military hospital for the next seven years.

It was not until January 1791 that it was again opened as an "Asylum for Pain and Distressed." Shortly thereafter the State Legislature changed the name of the governing body to its present form. In 1798 the governors announced that the hospital was an infirmary and should receive only such persons as needed medical treatment or chirurgical management, lying-in women, and the insane needing special service. The New York Hospital was one of the first, if not the first, in America to open itself to clinical instruction—for "no instruction in the practice of medicine and surgery is worth the name that is not clinical."

CHAPTER XIII

During the Revolution

By 1776 the Revolutionary War was being fought with vigor, and everyone on Manhattan Island was involved. The first plan of the British was to gain control of the Hudson River and in this way cut New England off from the other colonies. One British army was to move down from Canada while another, under Lord Howe, was to capture New York City, then held by General Washington.

Howe had a much larger army than Washington, supported by a large fleet, and hoped to capture the Colonial troops stationed on Long Island. The Americans were defeated in the Battle of Long Island on August 29, 1776, but Washington, under cover of darkness, hurriedly collected boats on the Brooklyn side of the East River opposite Fulton Ferry and transported his small army of some nine thousand to Manhattan without the loss of a man. From the Fulton Street Ferry the army moved slowly northward on the old road that is now Pearl Street to the vicinity of the fresh-water lake. There they found an ample supply of water, rested and regrouped, and then proceeded up the Bowery to mid-Manhattan, opposite Kips Bay on the East River.

(In connection with Washington's retreat from Long Island, it should be noted that Brooklyn had its beginning November 26, 1646, as the village of Breuckelen, although the first settlement on the site was in 1636. The first ferry service from New Amsterdam to Long Island was established in 1646 near Fulton Street, the route used by Washington. Brooklyn became a city in 1834, when it absorbed about twenty-five villages, and a borough of New York City in 1898.)

45

The patriots fortified Collect Pond, the swamps in the area forming strategic lines. There was a powder plant near the intersection of Pearl and Elk Streets on the lower shores of the pond. A stone bridge had been built to carry Broadway over the canal (now Canal Street), and this bridge was fortified. The entire area around what is now Worth Street was organized in defense against the coming British attack.

Washington made his headquarters at the Morris Mansion, the home of Colonel Roger Morris, who had married the daughter of Frederick Philipse. (The Morris Mansion was occupied as a tavern for a short period after the Revolution, and was then purchased by Stephen Jumel, a Frenchman, whose widow married Aaron Burr.)

The British fleet finally moved up the East River to Kips Bay and landed an army. Washington moved his small force to Harlem Heights, a strong point which he felt could be defended against the combined land and sea forces of the British. Manhattan itself was vulnerable; because of its narrow width the British fleet could rake it from shore to shore. The Harlem River not only afforded Washington protection from the British ships but at Kingsbridge he had a passage into Westchester County if a retreat became necessary. A stand was made at Harlem Heights to regroup and secure reinforcements for the long campaign ahead. Later Washington did retire into Westchester to avoid being cut off.

The British occupied lower Manhattan, from the Worth Street area to the Battery, from September 15, 1776, to November 23, 1783. Most of the buildings suffered damage in one form or another. Soldiers vandalized homes, horses were quartered in churches, prisoners were confined in sugar factories, industrial buildings, and prison ships. The hospital became a British army barracks. During the occupation most of the patriots either moved away or were forced from their homes. Some joined the Continental Army, while others scattered to unoccupied areas. Many Tory families from other sections moved in and took over some of the vacated houses.

On September 21, 1776, a great fire destroyed five hundred buildings between the Battery and St. Paul's Church, and in 1778 a second fire destroyed three hundred more buildings in the lower Pearl Street area.

The British troops finally left New York on November 25, 1783, and on the same day General Washington marched into the city. He had been encamped in a field which is now the northern part of Central Park. The triumphant little band marched down the Bowery with Governor Clinton and crossed what is now Worth Street to the "Teawater Pump at Fresh-Water." There they were met by a delegation from the Battery who had marched up the "Broad-Way."

Leaving the Worth Street area, the "Order of Procession" for Washington and his army was as follows:

> A Party of Horse will precede their Excellencies and be on their flanks. After the General and Governor, will follow the Lieutenant-governor and Members of the Council for the temporary Government of the Southern Parts of the State. The Gentlemen on Horse-back, eight in front, those on Foot, in the Rear of the Horse, in like manner. Their Excellencies, after passing down Queen Street, and the line of Troops up the Broad-Way, will alight at Cape's Tavern. The Committee hope to see their Fellow-Citizens conduct themselves with Decency and Decorum on this joyful occasion.

The formal entry of Washington into New York City gave great hopes to the sorely tried patriots who had suffered British occupation for seven years. Now they could begin rebuilding their city after the devastation of fire and war.

When Washington returned in 1789, to be inaugurated as the first President of the United States, he stepped upon the balcony of Federal Hall in Wall Street clad in a suit of clothes made from cloth produced at the Hartford Manufactory in Hartford, Connecticut. Thus the first President, in his first official act, encouraged the domestic textile industry.

Chapter XIV

Early Days Under the Stars and Stripes

When the Revolution ended, the little city of New York resumed life with added vigor. Great plans were afoot. Collect Pond was in the news. In 1796 John Fitch demonstrated a model of his steamboat on the fresh-water lake. Soon Robert Fulton was to revolutionize harbor, river, and ocean transportation with steam.

Collect Pond was finally filled in to make way for the northern growth of the city, in 1808. In 1810 Canal Street was laid out. This street owes its name to the canal, about eight feet wide, that carried the waters of Lispenard Creek down its center. In 1819 the canal was covered and by 1840, when the street was resurfaced, it became nothing more than a drainage sewer.

But it is significant that Collect Pond delayed the growth of the city northward for many years. It was very popular for fishing in summer and skating in winter. The people were reluctant to give up their recreation grounds. The springs which supplied water to the pond have not surrendered. All attempts to block their flow have failed. Engineers state that if the walls of the present-day I.R.T. subway under Lafayette Street, from Worth to Canal Streets, were pierced, water would still gush forth. At this point the subway is built directly through the old lake bed, and not all of the water is carried away by the Canal Street aqueduct.

Early in the history of New York City a plot of about twenty-five acres was cleared on the east side of Broadway for use as a community grazing ground. This became known as the Common, or the Field, and is the present City Hall Park. In 1800 it was decided to build a City Hall on the old Common, and the building, still the seat of city government, was completed in 1815.

A map of 1789 shows Warren Street as the last named street to the north. Chapel (West Broadway) and Church Streets extended only to Reade Street. Broadway was laid out to the hospital, and was known above the Common as Great St. George's Street. Eight years later, a map of 1797 shows Chambers and Reade Streets named. Barley (Duane), Thomas, Catherine (Worth) and Leonard Streets had been laid out, as well as Catherine Lane, Magazine (Pearl) and Ann (Elm) Streets. Chapel and Church Streets, as well as Broadway, extended to Leonard Street.

Catherine (Worth) Street became Anthony Street in 1803, and other streets were authorized north to Canal Street. A map of 1808 shows the new streets of Sugar Loaf (Franklin), White, Walker and Lispenard. Canal Street was still a swamp. Sugar Loaf Street was undoubtedly named after the New York Sugar Refinery at the northwest corner of this street and Church.

The hospital buildings, and the gardens about them, were enclosed by a brick wall in 1801. By various acts of the State Legislature, large sums were annually provided for this institution. The fence around the property was not removed until 1827. The main building, with its handsome cupola, was in the center. The South Building was on the Duane Street side. On the other side were a laundry, a building for autopsies and lectures, and extensive stables.

The entrance to the hospital was seventy-five feet off Broadway and in line with the present Thomas Street. The North Hospital, a pavilion for one hundred beds, was erected in 1841 at approximately what is now the corner of Worth and Church Streets, the present Reeves Brothers corner.

The origins of the names of the streets that now are found in Worth Village reflect the early history of the city and the

nation. Franklin Street, was of course, named for Benjamin
Franklin; Duane Street for James Duane, the first mayor of
New York after the Revolution; Catherine Lane for the wife
of Hendricks Rutgers, who owned a farm near Chatham
Square.

Chambers Street was named for John Chambers, a lawyer
prominent in the city before the Revolution and the first legally
licensed attorney in the Province of New York who was a
native of the city. Lafayette Street was named for the Marquis
de Lafayette, who was visiting New York when the street was
opened. Chatham Square was named for William Pitt, the first
Earl of Chatham, who was very popular in America.

The Bowery, one of the oldest roads in the United States,
the first thoroughfare leading from the little city of New York
to the outside world, originally was a country lane running
from the present City Hall area to Peter Stuyvesant's *bowerie,*
the Dutch name for a country estate. The English named the
road Bowerie Lane. After the first post-rider traveled it in
1673 on the way to Boston, it was also known as the Boston
Post Road.

The Rutgers and Lispenard families were responsible for
many street names in the present Worth Street area. When
Leonard Lispenard married Elsie, the daughter of Anthony
Rutgers, in 1741, the great Rutgers Estate became the Lispenard Farm. Leonard Lispenard was an important man serving the city in various capacities. He had two sons, Anthony
and Leonard, and a daughter Cornelia, who married Thomas
Marston. It was from this family that Lispenard, Leonard,
Thomas and Anthony (later Worth) Streets derived their
names.

In the early 1800's the present Worth Street area was a fine
residential neighborhood with a thriving center of cultural life.
A row of residences was built on the west side of Broadway
between Anthony (Worth) Street and Leonard Street in 1807.
In 1815 residences were built up to Franklin Street, with only
a blacksmith shop to the north of them. But by 1820 resi-

dences lined Broadway as far as Canal Street, and expanded into the cross streets.

Contoits New York Garden was established in 1809 at the southwest corner of Broadway and Leonard Streets and soon became a popular roadhouse and eating place.

The eastern end of Anthony (Worth) Street, from Lafayette Street to Chatham Square, presented an entirely different picture. This section was the original "Land of the Werpoes." In the Indian era it was covered by the lake, swamps and lowlands. In time this land was drained and the lake filled in, but the land still was low and not suited to building purposes.

In 1800 this was north of the main city, and it became an area where the cheapest huts were built to house the riffraff of the times. The intersection of what is now Worth, Baxter and Park Streets was known as Five Points, and was the most disreputable section of the city from 1810 to 1830. Sleeping quarters were available in the cheapest lodging houses, grog shops infested the section, vice was rampant, and it was a formidable area inhabited by thieves and other criminals.

For a long period two rival gangs fought for the rule of the Five Points section, and they eventually became involved in politics. One was known as the Dead Rabbits and the other as the Bowery Boys. They not only fought among themselves but preyed upon the population over a wide area. By night the neighborhood was dark and dangerous, by day it was squalid and dreary. Every language of the globe was spoken there, and it was at the risk of life that one entered the section.

Today the old Five Points section is the civic center. On one corner is Columbus Park, and on the others are the large buildings owned by the city, county and state of New York. It is a transformation hardly believable—from the cheapest buildings to the finest modern structures. On the site of former crime and disorder has risen a new and dignified courthouse.

By 1823 the population of Manhattan had reached 150,000. From 1825 onward New York's horizons widened into the metropolitan concept of modern times. In contrast to Boston,

Philadelphia and other colonial settlements, New Amsterdam had been founded mainly for commercial reasons.

The opening of the Erie Canal in 1825 and the expansion of the West began the process which soon made New York the market place, the banking center, the gateway to the New World and finally the greatest city in the world.

CHAPTER XV

The First Half of the Nineteenth Century

Worth Village in the early nineteenth century was a precursor of the Manhattan of today. Great authors, song-writers and actors lived and worked there, famous preachers and fiery orators thundered their convictions, and at least one very popular magazine of the times was published in the neighborhood.

The Anthony Street Theater was built prior to 1817 at 79-81-83 Anthony (Worth) Street. During the summer of 1817 the Park Street Theater used it for a ballet and circus. Edmund Kean, the great English tragedian and leading Shakespearean actor of his day, made his debut there in 1820 in *Richard III* after the famous Park Street Theater, where he had expected to play, burned down. The latter was rebuilt by John Jacob Astor in 1821.

In the 1830's the National Theater was located at the northwest corner of Church and Leonard Streets. Still later, from 1847 to 1859, the Old Broadway, a popular playhouse, stood at 326-330 Broadway, between Pearl and Anthony (Worth) Streets.

Thomas A. Cooper, another famous English actor and the acknowledged greatest Hamlet of his day, lived at 350 Broadway in the early 1800's. Cooper was the idol of literary men of his age, including Washington Irving, who apparently was no stranger to the early village of Worth.

A literary curiosity associated with the Worth Street district concerns Edgar Allan Poe. While Poe is not known ever to have visited Worth Village, yet one of his best-known

53

stories is associated with it. More than a century ago, in 1841, a young girl named Mary Cecilia Rogers lived with her mother on Nassau Street. She was employed in a cigar shop at 321 Broadway (corner of Thomas Street) owned by John Anderson, who lived at 52 White Street. Mary was murdered and her body was found in the Hudson near Weehawken. The murder was one of the great sensations of the time and was the principal topic of discussion in the newspapers. It was in an era of personal journalism, and editors suggested all sorts of solutions, while berating the police for their failure to capture the murderer. In November 1842 the crime was still unsolved when Edgar Allan Poe published his *Mystery of Marie Roget,* using the characters and most of the background of the Mary Rogers case but transferring its locale to Paris. Poe's fictional detective, Auguste Dupin, proceeded to solve the crime. Not long afterward the Rogers case was actually solved, guilt being established remarkably along the lines of Poe's story.

John Howard Payne, author of the immortal "Home, Sweet Home," made his headquarters at the picture shop of Charles H. Brainerd, which was at 347 Broadway, the southwest corner of Broadway and Leonard Streets, in 1851. It was from this spot that Payne set out for his last trip from home. He had accepted a second appointment as American consul at Tunis in North Africa, where he died in 1852.

Jenny Lind, the Swedish nightingale, arrived in the autumn of 1850 on the *S. S. Atlantic,* which docked at Canal Street. P. T. Barnum of circus fame had brought her to New York, and with publicity had created great interest in the visit. Huge crowds lined Broadway, so thick at the corner of Anthony (Worth) Street that the procession was delayed in reaching the Irving Hotel at the corner of Chambers Street and Broadway, where 20,000 New Yorkers had assembled to greet her. Seats for her concert held at Castle Garden sold at auction as high as $225. (Castle Garden was on a small rock island off the toe of Manhattan, one of the island rocks in a group known as the Kapsee Islands belonging to the old Manahatta Village.)

Another well-known man who formerly lived in the Worth Street area was John Ericsson, the designer of the famous navy ship *Monitor* of Civil War days and also the inventor of the propeller for steamships. His home was on the corner of Church and Franklin Streets. A plaque has been erected at this point with the following inscription:

CAPTAIN JOHN ERICSSON,
Resided here at 95 Franklin Street 1844-1864.
He designed in 1861, the first iron clad turreted battleship,

"MONITOR"

The contract was obtained from the government by Cornelius S. Bushnell of New Haven, Conn., who, with John F. Winslow and John A. Griswold of Troy, N.Y., financed its construction. It was built in 100 working days. On March 9, 1862 the "Monitor" under John L. Worden, Commander, Alban C. Stimers, Chief Engineer, arrived at Hampton Roads, Va., and after a severe engagement, ended the career of the "Merrimac" which on the preceding day had sunk the U.S.S. "Cumberland" and "Congress." The tide of the war was turned and the design of the "Monitor" revolutionized the navies of the world.

Robert Fulton, the inventor of the steamboat, had earlier (1809) lived in the Worth Street area, at 100 Reade Street.

The first hotel erected in Worth Village was at the corner of Chambers Street and West Broadway. Now known as the Bond Hotel, and before that the Cosmopolitan, it is one of the oldest hotel buildings in the city today, if not the oldest. The original hotel on this site was opened in 1850 under the name of the Gerard House, although the present building was erected in 1868. The Gerard House drew a steady patronage in its early days from the steamship piers and the first Hudson River Railroad Terminal, which was across the street.

Fine "eating houses and refectories" abounded in Worth Village in the early days. Taylor's New Restaurant and Hotel at Broadway and Franklin Streets was described as "perhaps the most elegant and extensive establishment of its kind in the world." The front of this building was constructed of brownstone, newly fashionable then, ornamented in the richest manner. There was a frontage of fifty feet on Broadway, and one hundred and fifty feet on Franklin Street. The grand saloon, the ceiling of which was nearly twenty feet in height, covered an area of seventy-five hundred square feet.

Operating today, only a few blocks south of Worth Village at 118 Cedar Street, is Ye Olde Chop House, which was built in 1800 as "Old Tom's." It is a colorful place where good food is served in an atmosphere of old New York, surrounded by hundreds of historic pictures and mementos. Many of the old-time textile merchants dined there around 1850 when that area was the textile center.

The famous Gem Saloon in 1853 was at 324 Broadway, close to Worth Street. This was the political headquarters of the day.

In 1850 the Broadway Bank was at 336 Broadway (corner of Worth Street), and the Bowling Saloon was at 314-316 Broadway.

In 1869 there was a gold refinery at the northeast corner of Thomas Street and West Broadway, and the Union Steam Sugar Refinery at the southwest corner of Leonard Street and West Broadway in the days when Worth Street was "sugar" and "gold."

Putnam's Monthly, a famous periodical of its time, was published on Worth Street just west of Broadway.

The hospital furnished its own element of excitement. The police were called to quell a serious riot when the students were accused of "body snatching"—exhuming bodies from the city cemeteries for the purpose of studying anatomy. Feelings ran high, and for a few days physicians feared to travel the streets. But this too passed over.

Such was the Worth Village neighborhood of the first half of the nineteenth century.

CHAPTER XVI

The Churches of Worth Village

In the early 1800's the Worth Street area was a popular location for churches of various denominations, and it soon became a hallowed spot in the minds of people throughout the lower section of Manhattan.

During the Dutch and early English eras the churches of Manhattan were somewhat crudely equipped and most were rather bleak places. People were supposed to go to church to seek religion rather than comfort. The church buildings were generally closed during the week in winter and opened only on Sundays—one record states that they were "cold enough to freeze the milk of human kindness in every bosom." Regardless of all this, most people went to church on Sundays. Churches gradually became more elaborate in their buildings, and new churches were built in the thriving residential section.

A Congregational church was located between Warren and Chambers Streets, near Broadway. Zion Church was between Mott and Mulberry Streets; a Methodist church was on Barclay Street west of West Broadway, and a Universalist church was near Pearl Street and Park Row.

St. Peter's Church at Barclay and Church Streets is the oldest Roman Catholic Church in the city. It was founded in 1785, and the present building was erected in 1836.

According to a map of New York dated 1808, the old African Methodist Church was located at the southwest corner of what is now Church and Leonard Streets.

. The "new" Scots Presbyterian Church was on Pearl Street

between Broadway and Elm, while the Reformed Scots Church was on Chambers Street, also between Broadway and Elm.

Christ Protestant Episcopal Church was erected in 1822 upon a plot of ground consisting of 75 to 83 Worth Street. This was formerly the site of the old Anthony Street Theatre. The church had earlier been located on Ann Street. The edifice was a handsome gray and brown stone building in Gothic style. When it burned in 1847 the congregation temporarily used the Minerva Rooms at 406 Broadway until a new building was completed in 1848. In 1853, however, the building was abandoned "due to the influx of business in the area," and the church moved to Eighteenth Street.

The Broadway Tabernacle was erected at 95-103 Worth Street in 1836. The entrance was at 340 Broadway. It was originally called the Sixth Free Presbyterian Church, but by 1850 had become a Congregational church. It was from the pulpit of the Broadway Tabernacle that Wendell Phillips preached, and from which the abolitionist William Lloyd Garrison sought to arouse New Yorkers on the issue of slavery.

Anthony (Worth) Street made the front pages in the autumn of 1853 when the Women's Rights Convention convened for two days in the auditorium of the Broadway Tabernacle. The convention excited the city and a large part of the nation. It was attended by women delegates from a wide area, some of whom were already notorious or famous, according to one's viewpoint, as agitators for women's rights. Among the delegates were Miss Susan B. Anthony, Miss Lucy Stone, Mrs. Elizabeth Stanton, and others of equal rank in this cause.

They were campaigning not only for the right to vote but for general equality with men. It was at this convention in 1853 that Miss Lucy Stone, to publicize their cause and to defy tradition, wore a daring costume of a short skirt above long bloomers. The attire was considered scandalous at the time and caused a sensation. The convention was quite boisterous. It upset the quiet, staid traditions of the residential area, and at one point was quieted by the police. This historic convention on Anthony (Worth) Street had a far-reaching effect on dress and the trend of textiles just as the Street was becoming a textile center. By coincidence, this convention was held on the actual site of the old Indian village of Manahatta, where Indian women were a power in tribal thinking, ran the households and did most of the work, leaving only the fighting to the men.

In 1853 the Dutch Reformed Church was at 107-113 Franklin Street, while the Abyssinian Baptist Church was at 44-46 Worth Street.

At the eastern end of Worth Street is historic Chatham Square, which has ten streets radiating from it. Close by that end of Worth Street is Chinatown, and surrounding it are many old buildings of historical and sentimental value.

In this area is Mariners' Temple, one of the most fascinating churches in New York, and the oldest Baptist Church on Manhattan Island. The original building was erected in 1795. After its destruction by fire, the present edifice was built in 1914, in the Greek Revival style of architecture with Corinthian columns. The building is owned by the Baptist Home Mission Society. The church bell, still on exhibition, formerly called seamen from the East River to services. Mariners' Temple has been called the Mother of Churches because of the number of churches organized within it. In 1867 the First Swedish Baptist Church was organized here, followed by the First Italian Baptist Church in 1894, the First Russian Baptist Church in 1916, and in 1926 the First Chinese Baptist Church. The Temple site, Oliver and Henry Streets, "was given in 1729 by Noe Willey of London to be a place of burial for the Jewish Nation forever." The plot was sold, however, and since 1795 has been the site of Mariners' Temple.

Chinatown developed on the north side of Worth Street in the Chatham Square area and is today a mecca for visitors.

In the rear of 195 Worth Street is the True Light Chinese Lutheran Church. It is beautifully decorated and well worth a visit. Red, the Chinese color of happiness, dominates the chancel hangings and focuses the eye upon the altar cross. The altar is executed in green marble that calls to mind precious jade. The church has a small prayer room with a key hanging beside the door which may be used to insure complete privacy. A tablet on the door states that the room is reserved for "those who want to talk things over with God and pray alone."

In this church an Oriental legend is quoted:

> A Chinese photographer was riding one day through the snow-covered countryside of interior China. His soul was troubled. He had been witnessing a great move toward Christianity among his friends since the Japanese invasion. He longed to know the truth of what he had been hearing from Christian missionaries. As he rode along, he said, "Lord, if I could only see Thy face, I would believe." Instantly a voice spoke to his heart, "Take a picture! Take a picture!" He looked out at the melting snow, forming pools of water and revealing here and there the black earth. It was an unattractive scene. Nevertheless, being thus strangely compelled, the man descended and focused his camera on the snowy roadside. Curious to know the outcome of the incident, he developed the film at once on returning home. Out from among the black and white areas of the snow scene a Face looked at him, full of tenderness and love—the face of Christ. He became a Christian as the result. And because the Chinese people think that God has in this wonderful way revealed Himself to them in the hour of their trial, many have since found the Saviour through the picture, as the story of it is told in various parts of China.

CHAPTER XVII

Trade Enters Worth Village

As early as 1848 it became apparent that Worth Village was destined to become a great trade area. In that year A. T. Stewart built New York's first large department store at the corner of Chambers Street and Broadway. It was a magnificent marble structure and when it opened it was declared to be the largest dry goods store in the world.

During its colorful career its name was never placed outside the building; the store was so well known that this was considered unnecessary. It was a six-story "marble palace" with fifteen immense plate glass windows. Two hundred clerks were employed. It became the fashion and shopping center, and was operated with great success.

The store started a modern trend of life in Manhattan. After shopping the ladies strolled along Broadway to Franklin Street, where John Taylor had erected a brilliantly trimmed ice cream parlor, a place where, for the first time in New York's history, ladies were served even though not escorted by gentlemen. This was a daring but successful experiment. Ice cream and pastries, as well as the merchandise offered, attracted ladies to the new shopping center.

With the Worth Street area established as a retail dry goods center, the wholesale merchants began looking toward the neighborhood for permanent business locations.

For a period of two centuries—from 1635 to 1835—the textile trading center of Manhattan was a coordinated market place on lower Pearl Street. The district was firmly established near the docks where imports arrived. Then came the great fire of 1835, which destroyed the entire district overnight and made it necessary for the textile merchants to find new homes. After the fire some firms settled in Broad, Liberty and Cedar Streets, and later in Fulton and Murray Streets. From the very beginning of textile trade in Manhattan, two centuries ago, merchants had recognized that it was desirable for them to have one center where competitors would be in close touch with one another and buyers would enjoy a central market place.

After some twenty years of disorganization in scattered locations, the textile merchants realized that they must again concentrate in a district of their own.

Other factors were at work, since the wholesale market in textiles was taking on new responsibilities. Methods of trading were changing. In the years between 1825 and 1835 auctions in the textile district on Pearl Street were quite common and considered the most satisfactory method for quickly distributing textiles arriving from abroad. Often cargoes were larger than could be readily financed by the importing firm. In addition to all this, domestic textiles were beginning to come to New York in increasing quantities.

When the textiles merchants decided, in 1853, to concentrate in the Worth Street area, they passed over several other possible districts. The Worth Street area presented many advantages, it was already a retail center and it was convenient to all points in the city, which was expanding northward at a great rate.

Finally, an additional factor made the Worth Street area particularly attractive. The New York Hospital grounds offered a wide expanse of space upon which new buildings might be erected. Events followed which benefited both the hospital and the merchants seeking a market place.

In 1857, shortly after the first textile merchants had come to Worth Street, it so happened that the appropriations from the State to the New York Hospital ceased by legislative limitation. The city refused to grant assistance, and private donations and bequests were withheld through a determination on the part of the public to force the governors of the institution to lease or sell the valuable grounds. There were a variety of cases crowding the hospital. In 1860 the comment was made that the hospital was receiving so many accident cases from the crowded thoroughfare Broadway, and from the busy shipping and machinery industries, that its facilities were overtaxed. By 1868 the hospital had gone into debt to the extent of $100,000, and in 1869 the governors decided to lease the grounds of the main building and the North Hospital. The patients were moved to the South Hospital. The institution, with a bed capacity of 500, continued in use until 1869, when the main building was demolished and Thomas Street cut through the grounds from Church Street to Broadway as a private thoroughfare.

The Hospital Society had found the maintenance of the old structure too costly now that a business section had grown up around it where property values were so high. They finally bought a large plot of land between 15th and 16th Streets, off Fifth Avenue; a new hospital was built in 1875.

On February 16, 1869, by order of the "Committee of the Governors of the Society of the New York Hospital," Adrian H. Muller and P. R. Wilkins, auctioneers, offered for sale a lease of fifty parcels, including a large plot on Church Street between Duane and the proposed Thomas Street. While 317 and 319 Broadway were included in this sale, other Broadway frontage was not, probably because the Society had already sold these lots.

Most of this leasehold came under control of the New York Real Estate Association, which was organized under a charter granted May 27, 1869, through an act passed in 1853 known as Chapter 117. This Association was composed largely of merchants who desired to make this a wholesale woolen and cotton goods center for the firms then scattered over a wide area from Fulton to White Streets. The law allowed only a capital of $500,000 for an organization of this character.

Since the buildings to be erected on the lots leased by the Hospital Society were estimated to cost at least one million dollars, another $500,000 was added as "surplus" to make up the full amount.

The buildings on the block between Church Street and Broadway, Thomas and Worth Streets, were erected by Griffith Thomas "for the flourishing textile trade in which many of the wealthiest citizens of New York were engaged. They represent the florid architectural style of the post-Civil War period when structural feats impossible in stone were accomplished with the use of cast iron." The cast iron was used as a facing on the front, the basic construction being of heavy brick and wood. At first only the three lower floors of the six were plastered; the upper floors were used for storage. The historic value of these buildings lies in their close association with textiles for nearly a century.

Each of these buildings has a history of its own. For instance, the records show that the leasehold on two parcels, 54/56 Worth Street and 39/41 Thomas Street, now controlled by Reeves Brothers, was originally taken by James F. White & Co., then in the cotton and linen business. The lease for the fronts on Worth and Thomas Streets was signed April 20, 1869, by James F. White and Bryce Grey, for a term of twenty-one years. The plans for the construction of the building were filed June 8, 1869. They called for a building 86½ feet high, six stories, with frontages on Worth and Thomas Streets of 34 feet each, and a full frontage of 180 feet 5 inches on Church Street. The front of the building was specified as an "Iron Wall." These plans were filed in the name of Bryce Grey, a member of the firm of James F. White & Co., the leaseholder. The architects were William Field and Son. The builder and mason were Moore and Bryant; the carpenters, Jas. C. Hoe & Co., and the iron work was done by the Architectural Iron Works. The estimated cost of labor and materials was $175,000, and the building was completed on February 8, 1870.

In 1887 another lease was taken by Bryce Grey, James F. White, James M. White and others. On April 17, 1890, still another lease, apparently for twenty-one years also, was signed by the executors of the estates of James F. White and Alex. F. White. On January 10, 1910, the James F. White interests again renewed this leasehold for twenty-one years. In the meantime, White, Lamb & Finlay, Inc., took over the interests of James F. White & Co. and Lamb, Finlay & Co. In 1936 this latter company took another lease of twenty-one years. In December 1946 the Charles F. Noyes Company, acting as broker, sold the leasehold to the New York Hospital. At that time Reeves Brothers and certain subtenants took over the building on a lease from the hospital authorities.

As for the other lots in this block: lots covering Nos. 58/60 to 82/84 Worth Street and 35/37 to 11/13 Thomas Street were taken as leasehold by the New York Real Estate Association. Nos. 86/88 Worth Street and 9/7 Thomas Street were originally leased to H. Bauendal & Co., who sold to Lewis Bros. & Co., who in turn sold to the New York Real Estate Association on May 1, 1891. Eleven buildings were constructed on the seven lots 58/60 to 82/84 Worth Street, which run through to Thomas Street. This offered a total frontage of 275 feet and a depth of 180 feet. On four alternate lots, two buildings were constructed on each lot with a courtyard twenty-four feet wide between. The plans for this group were filed May 13, 1869, calling for structures about 39 feet 3 inches wide and six stories high. The estimated cost for the group was $700,000. The owner is noted as S. D. Babcock, trustee; the architect was Griffith Thomas, said to have been the outstanding man in his profession at the time, and the builders were Stewart and Smith. Work started on August 23, 1869, and was completed, according to departmental records, on May 14, 1870.

The large plot between Thomas and Duane Streets facing Church Street was acquired as a leasehold by the Manhattan Real Estate Association. Two other plots in this block, between Thomas and Duane Streets, Nos. 8 and 10 Thomas Street through to Duane Street, were subsequently acquired by the lessees.

For some time after 1870, part of the hospital buildings were left standing at the southwest corner of the hospital property. About 1872 the New York Real Estate Association complained about the condition of the property as being "very detrimental to adjoining property." So, on December 22, 1873, a lease was made by the Hospital Society to the Manhattan Real Estate Association covering the properties 18 to 40 Thomas Street and 109 to 133 Duane Street, the lot just referred to.

In erecting buildings on their property, the Manhattan Real Estate Association left uncovered a strip of about thirty-eight feet in the middle of the plot, now Trimble Place, which gave light, air and private shipping facilities to the buildings. A large steam plant was built under the corner of Thomas Street and Trimble Place. It is still there, but no longer used.

On July 1, 1929, the New York Real Estate Association and the Manhattan Real Estate Association sold all of their buildings and leaseholds to the Broadway Church Street Corporation.

An old report in the files of the New York Hospital by an executive officer states: "From 1869 to 1929 there has never been a 10% vacancy in any of the buildings owned by the New York Real Estate Association and the Manhattan Real Estate Association and we have never missed a quarterly dividend during the entire period in either company. During the period they returned more than $25,000,000 in rent, and loss of rent due to business failure amongst the tenants did not exceed $10,000."

In 1935 the Broadway Church Street Corporation sold all the holdings of this company back to the New York Hospital. With this transaction the New York Hospital again controlled the property on Worth Street from numbers 54 to 88; on Thomas Street from 7 to 41 and from 8 to 40; on Duane

Street from 101 to 133; and numbers 317 and 319 on Broadway. In 1948 all these properties, including the land titles of the Hospital Society, were acquired from the New York Hospital by Charles F. Noyes and associates, who, in turn, sold the land and buildings to textile firms in the area. Thus, for a period of one hundred and seventy-six years—from 1772 to 1948—title to this large and valuable tract rested with one of New York's most important philanthropic institutions, and the revenues contributed to its role in the history of Manhattan. From its very inception the hospital's Board of Governors included outstanding citizens who helped shape the destiny of the nation as well. Often referred to as the "Mother of Hospitals," New York Hospital, today a part of the great Cornell Medical Center, is world-famous for its many-faceted services to humanity and to the advancement of science.

CHAPTER XVIII

The Crossroads of Worth

Broadway is not only one of the world's most famous streets but also one of its oldest highways. For centuries men have trod this thoroughfare, which may well be older than some of the historic avenues of Rome. And even before men followed the path, animals traced it seeking the source of life—the fresh-water lake.

The most used of all the Indian trails that led to Lake Manahatta was the Kapsee Trail, which ran north and south along the center of the island like a backbone. Apparently the instincts of the animals that determined its course led them along the elevated center ridge, where they could sense any danger that might lurk on either slope. It was popular with the Indians for the same reason, and also because it was the shortest distance between the Indian settlement of Kapsee on the southern tip of the island and the land area to the north. This great Indian highway was gradually broadened by the Dutch and the English, and finally became the main artery through the village of Worth—the backbone of the City of New York and one of the world's most celebrated streets.

It is a route which has had many names in its long and varied career. The lower portion has been called in the various eras the Kapsee Trail, the Weckquaeskeck Trail, the Center Trail, Heere Waage, Wag Briedweg, the Great Public Road, the Public Highway, the Great Highway, the Common Highway, the Broad Wagon Way, Broad Way and finally Broadway. To the north of the village of Worth it has, at various times, been known as the Sappokanican Trail, Great George Street,

68

Middle Road, Boston Road, Bloomingdale Road, Manhattan-
ville Road and Kingsbridge Road. An old map of 1808 shows
Broad Way as the name of the route from the Battery up to
about 10th Street. From 10th to 147th Street the route was
called Bloomendale Road; and from there to King's Bridge,
at the Harlem River, it was known as the King's Bridge Road.

Another old trail, the Wampum or Southeastern Trail, led
from the settlement of Manahatta to the East River and along
its shore south to Kapsee, a circuitous water-level route. Eventually the Dutch settled along the lower portion of this trail
in the meadow lands along the East River, and the trail became known as Pearl Street. This name was derived from the
pearly shells found along the shores, and Pearl Street today
has the distinction of being the oldest named street in the city.
The southern end of Pearl Street in its beginning as a trail
originated near the spot that also marked the start of the
Kapsee Trail. By a meandering route northward it finally
joined the Kapsee Trail again in the present village of Worth.
This is the only street in New York following just such a
pattern.

The great Western, or Lapinikin, Trail led from Manahatta
to the shores of the Hudson, forming a connecting link with
the tribes across the river in what is now New Jersey, and even
farther west to the Delaware River and Pennsylvania. This
trail passed through the Indian village of Lapinikin on the
east bank of the Hudson. The village was located at the mouth
of Lapinikin, later Lispenard, Creek at a site not far from the
present Holland Tunnel. The first "ferry" across the Hudson
was established by the Indians at Lapinikin.

The Northern, or Sappokanican, Trail first circled around
the southern end of the lake, over a route that is now Pearl
Street, and then led north over a route that is now the Bowery.
This old trail was sometimes called the Weckquaeskeck Trail
because it led northward to the land of the Weckquaeskecks,
now Westchester County. It was later known as the "road to
the Bouwrie," and still later as the Bowerie Lane and the

Bowery Road. In time this became the "road to Boston" and then the Boston Post Road, the oldest post road on Manhattan Island. When it became the Boston Post Road, stone mile markers were erected on it from City Hall, across Worth Street, to the northern tip of the Island and on to Boston.

The Eastern, or Rechtanck, Trail followed the Sappokanican Trail until it reached what is now Chatham Square, and then turned eastward to the East River in the vicinity of Marginnoe or Corlear's Hook. This trail was an important route for the Indians of Long Island in reaching Manahatta and passing on to other villages to the west and across the Hudson. It followed the route of East Broadway, which in 1808 was known as Harmon Street. Even today Worth Street is the connecting link between East Broadway, Broadway and West Broadway.

As time passed, the Worth Street area continued to be the crossroads of activity for ever-expanding Manhattan. Commerce soon forced the population northward, and transportation began to be a highly complicated problem. Carriages of many types were to be seen. As the city expanded, more and more local stagecoach lines were put in operation, some coaches being drawn by four horses.

It was estimated that at one time over twenty thousand people used these stage lines daily, most of them passing through the Worth Street district from their residences to the north to their offices to the south. The busiest period was at noon, when the merchants went home for their midday dinner.

The railroad came to the village of Worth in 1831, when the New York and Harlem Railroad began operation. Its southern terminus was No. 1 Tryon Row, which was approximately at the present intersection of Park Row and Center and Chambers Streets. It crossed the present Worth Street on Center Street and followed that route north. It was the first railroad on Manhattan Island, and the cars were drawn by horses. Later an important freight yard and depot were built at Center and White Streets. The upper depot was at 26th Street and Fourth Avenue, on the site of the old Madison Square Garden.

Its next terminal was at the site of the present Grand Central Station, and by 1844 the railroad was constructed on to White Plains.

On the west, the Hudson River Railroad entered the Worth Street district in 1847. Its original passenger station was built on Chambers Street near West Broadway, at the edge of the village of Worth. Its route was up Hudson Street to Canal Street, to West Street and thence to Tenth Avenue. The coaches were drawn by horses to the northern terminal at Tenth Avenue and West 31st Street. It was finally extended to Spuyten Duyvil, Yonkers and Albany.

The Camden and Amboy Railroad, which later was to become the Pennsylvania Railroad, was opened to Perth Amboy, New Jersey, in 1834. Connections from there to its terminus on Manhattan Island were made by means of steamboats operating on regular schedules.

Thus it will be seen that the village of Worth was the first railroad center on Manhattan Island.

The first bridge in the Worth Street area was probably a single log over the small stream, Old Wreck Brook, flowing from Manahatta Lake to the East River. This was on the Rechtanck Trail. But the first bridge of which there is definite record was of stone, erected about 1776 to carry Broadway over the canal to the undeveloped areas to the north.

The first bridge connecting Manhattan Island with the mainland was King's Bridge at the northern end of the island, over the Harlem River, erected by Frederick Philipse as a toll bridge with a charter from the King of England in 1693.

Partly to take care of the ever-expanding activities of the crossroads, the great Brooklyn Bridge was constructed in the latter part of the nineteenth century. It was completed May 24, 1883, after thirteen years of work and the expenditure of $25,000,000. From the day of its opening it has been one of the leading traffic arteries into the village of Worth. The Brooklyn Bridge replaced the once-popular Fulton Street Ferry, the route of Washington's army across the East River, which in turn had superseded the old Indian ferry leading from the Wampum Trail to the Canarsie Indian country, now Brooklyn.

Later the Manhattan Bridge was built, forming another vital artery into the Worth Street area on the north, where it enters Canal Street. This bridge is today a busy thoroughfare handling much of the crossroads traffic between Long Island and New Jersey, taking the modern place of the Indian Rechtanck Trail.

Still later the Holland Tunnel was constructed under the Hudson from a spot near the Lapinikan Ferry of the Indians, permitting rapid transit with the west. The tunnel roughly follows the course of the old Lapinikan Trail and its ferry.

As ocean traffic increased, docks were built on the Hudson and East Rivers, and great ships from all parts of the world began to berth not far from the village of Worth. It is impossible to do justice in words to the great harbor of New York created by the Hudson and East Rivers—there is no other harbor just like it. It is well protected from the storms of the sea, and is so vast that it can accommodate the ships of the world without crowding. The greatest liners sail into the harbor directly from the ocean and land with ease at the docks, some of which are only a few hundred yards from the village of Worth.

The surface railroads disappeared with the building of the Pennsylvania Station and the Grand Central Terminal, and were succeeded by surface streetcar lines which crossed the village of Worth at several places. These, in turn, were replaced by bus lines and rapid-transit subway lines, four of which now pass under the village. Two elevated lines at one time crossed the area.

The streets of the village were paved first with cobblestones and later with asphalt. Worth Street became a popular crosstown thoroughfare, while Broadway continued as an important artery paralleled by Lafayette Street on the east and Church Street on the west.

No story of transportation in the village of Worth, or New York itself, would be complete without mention of the elevator. The first elevator on Manhattan Island was a freight elevator built in Hecker's flour mill at 201 Cherry Street in 1851. Shortly thereafter passenger elevators were installed in the then new Fifth Avenue Hotel. The importance of the elevator in the development of New York cannot be overestimated. With vertical transportation added to horizontal, tall buildings could be erected and a great amount of activity could be concentrated within a limited number of square feet of street-level surface. Since greater numbers of people could use buildings in a limited area, the problem of transportation to carry these people to and from their homes increased.

Lying as it does at the center of the crossroads of the island, Worth Village has the advantage of being near many transportation routes, which permits those who work there to live in any section of the great metropolitan area.

Chapter XIX

Thirsty for Water

It may surprise Manhattanites to learn that for more than three centuries the history of their island has been one long search for water. The original inhabitants, the Indians, were far shrewder in this quest than the Dutch and English who followed.

The island, of solid rock formation, is practically surrounded by salt water, and fresh water is, and always has been, at a great premium. The Indians established their capital village of Manahatta beside the lake of fresh water, thus assuring themselves of an ample supply at all times. The Dutch, on the contrary, settled upon the tip of the island, where fresh water was indeed scarce.

There were some few springs scattered throughout the island which supplied the Indians with fresh water in addition to the lake. A parcel of ground 75 feet by 120 feet on the north side of Chatham Street (Park Row), beginning 28 feet east of Baxter Street, marks a site of great importance in the annals of Manhattan's search for water: the famous "Teawater Spring" of colonial days, the "Laughing Waters Spring" of the Indians.

The expanding city long ago erased all traces of the spring. But here in earlier days, near the southern shores of the fresh-water lake, was a small rocky dell surrounded by tall trees, with an outcropping of large boulders that cradled a shadowy pool fed by crystal-clear water bubbling from beneath the great rocks. The Indians were intrigued both by the setting and by the waters themselves as they tumbled along from boulder to boulder with a muffled sound which reverberated from the rocky walls. Their "Legend of the Laughing Waters," built around this spring, speaks of a trail along the happy waters which the Indian braves and girls trod from time immemorial in their quest for happiness. The Dutch, however, were too busy trying to establish a foothold on the toe of the island to travel a mile north to the enchanted spring of the Indians. In time, however, the English rediscovered the spring as they traveled up the old Indian trail which had become Bouwerie Lane. Soon the spring became famous again as Teawater Spring.

The springs and lakes of Manahatin were ample for the needs of the Indians, but with the coming of the Dutch, water became a problem. The island then began a search for water that passed through the eras of springs, wells, pumps and water carts, and finally reservoirs and world-famous aqueducts.

The first small Dutch band of some thirty settlers at the tip of the island depended upon the Indian spring near the Kapsee Trail, at about what is now Wall Street, for their supply. As the colony grew to two hundred, this spring still remained ample for their needs. But when the population reached one thousand it was necessary to seek water from a spring a little farther north, at what is now Maiden Lane. This street got its name from the Dutch maidens who did the family wash in the small stream and strolled on the path beside its shores.

When the English seized the island in 1664 they were surprised at the shortage of water in Fort Amsterdam, and found it necessary to unload barrels of water from their ships. In 1667, Governor Nicholls ordered that a well be dug on Broad Way at Bowling Green, and purely through chance he secured a small supply of fresh water by tapping a pocket of rainwater. This well—the first on the island—brought in an era of wells, the first manmade supply. Other wells were soon dug in the surrounding area, but they produced only brackish water unfit for human consumption. By 1709, when the population had reached 4000, water had become a serious problem. Many

more wells were dug, but most produced only seepage salt
water.

It must be remembered that this lower portion of the island
was, in effect, a turtleback—a high center sloping gradually
to the salt water on each side. There were no underground
rivers or deep springs coming to the surface. The only fresh
water to be found was in small soil pockets in the rocks above
the salt-water level, where rain was caught and stored. Not
many of these pockets existed, and the supply of fresh water
in each was limited.

In 1677, the Common Council made plans for the orderly
construction of wells. It ordered that "severall weels bee made
in the places hereafter menconed (for the publique good of
the Cytie) by the inhabitants of each Street where the said
weels shall be made viztt: . . ." The order goes on to designate
the locations of five wells, one of which (the first stone well
in the city) was in the back yard of the City Hall at 73 Pearl
Street. In 1686, the Council issued another order for nine more
wells to be built of stone, "one halfe of the charge of them to
be borne by the inhabitants of every street proportionately and
the other halfe by the Citty." This practice of dividing the expense continued as long as the public well system was used. A
citizen was appointed as guardian of each well. Many more
wells were dug, and the records show most of their locations,
such as Rombout's Well, at Broadway near Exchange Place,
and Wessel's Well, at Wall Street west of William Street.

The village continued to expand, and by 1737 was a city
of ten thousand, with houses concentrated near the tip of the
island. Up until this time a type of open well was generally
used similar to that in common use in the Old World. A bucket
was suspended from a rope or chain attached to one end of a
pole, supplied with a pivot and a weight on the opposite end
to counterbalance it.

The era of the pump arrived in the first half of the eighteenth
century. Soon the pump superseded the open well and its

bucket. The pumps became social centers where people met to gossip, and some became landmarks for the purpose of titles and deeds. The first pump was installed on the well at Bowling Green, and eventually most of them were named, usually after the owner of the land on which they were set up.

It became necessary to give thought to maintaining these public pumps and keeping them in repair. In 1741, the Assembly passed "an act for mending and keeping in repair the publick wells and pumps in the City of New York," and authorized the appointment of Overseers of Wells and Pumps, the levying of taxes for maintenance, and penalties for anyone damaging them. For the first time the city was in the water business, but with a very poor supply of water.

It is beyond comprehension that in 1737 ten thousand or more people were herded together in the lower tip of the island. The absence of any kind of a sewer system complicated matters: most of the wells, if not all, became contaminated. One old record mentions "tubbs of odour and nastiness" being dumped in the streets. These people for the most part suffered hardships, disease and even death before they would find a way to transport an ample supply of good water from the fresh-water lake only a mile distant.

The inevitable expansion of population forced people to the north until the city reached what is now City Hall Park. For the first time the fresh-water lake and its springs became interesting to white men as a water supply.

The water of the "Laughing Water Spring" of the Indians now came into use, and the name "Teawater Spring" was given to it. The name came from the fact that the water made excellent tea.

A visitor to the city in 1748 refers to the Teawater Spring:

> There is no good water to be met with in the town itself; but at a little distance there is a large spring of good water, which the inhabitants take for their tea and for the uses of the kitchen. Those, however, who are less

delicate on this point make use of the water from the
wells in town, though it be very bad. The want of good
water lies heavy upon the horses of strangers that come
to this place for they do not like to drink the water from
the wells of the town.

The water of this spring became so popular that selling it
expanded into a considerable business. Wagons hauled huge
hogsheads of it to the lower end of the island. Other carts
hauled it around town to sell by the cup or bucket.

These distributors were called "Teawater men," and became so numerous that in 1757 the Common Council passed
"a law for the regulating of Teawater men in the City of New
York." The number of these Teawater wagons became so great
on Chatham Street (Park Row) that they were causing con-
fusion and blocking traffic.

The big pump that had been installed at the spring was
equipped with an extra-long handle and spout which projected
over the street to facilitate the filling of wagons. Finally, in
1797, a petition was sent to the Common Council for an
abatement of the nuisance. It was referred to a committee,
which made the following report:

> The committee on the subject of the petition complain-
> ing of the obstruction in Chatham street caused by the
> Tea Water Pump delivering its water in the street and
> by the water carts drawn up across the street when about
> to receive water, report that they have viewed the prem-
> ises and find matters and things set forth in the petition
> true. That the committee have maturely considered the
> premises and are of the opinion that the said obstruction
> may be removed at no expense to Mr. Thompson, the
> present occupant and part proprietor of the premises, by
> causing the spout of the said pump to be raised about
> two feet and by lengthening it so as to deliver the water
> at the outer part of the paved walk, which would permit
> passengers to pass under without inconvenience; and if
> the water carts were ordered to draw up abreast of the
> spout near the gutter and receive the water in rotation it
> would remove the obstruction in the street.

The committee also recommended that the sidewalks in that vicinity be paved, but only the recommendations for the pump were approved.

Despite the Teawater wagons, many people still depended upon wells and pumps for water. The cost of digging early wells varied a great deal, depending on the depth and size and whether or not they were lined with stone. In 1783, a well and pump on Frankfort Street cost £80, one in the South Ward £9, while one on Catherine Street, near what is now Worth Street and Chatham Square, cost £30.

In 1785 one William Smith contracted to keep the wells and pumps in the city in repair for £140 per year. This proved unprofitable, because the number of wells was steadily increasing and the cost of repairs doubled.

The Common Council finally elected two Overseers of Pumps and Wells for each ward. They evidently were lax at times in performing their duties, for in 1789 the Common Council "ordered that whenever the overseers of Public Wells and Pumps neglect or refuse to do their duty that the Aldn and Assist of the Ward direct the necessary Repairs; lest by want of water from public wells and pumps the City may be endangered in case of fire." In 1789 the expense of such repairs amounted to £408:15:5½.

The delivery of water by wagon evidently started New Yorkers to thinking about the delivery of water to the consumer by some other means. In April 1774 Christopher Colles proposed a plan to build a reservoir near the Collect, or fresh-water lake, and then distribute the water through the streets from Canal Street to the Battery by means of underground pipes made from tree trunks with a hole bored lengthwise. These lengths of bored tree trunks were to be connected by joints. The water was to be pumped by steam from wells to be dug on the western shore of the lake, into a reservoir to be located on the hill between what is now Worth and White Streets on the east side of Broadway, then known as Great

George Street. From this elevated point the water was to flow
by gravity through pipes south to the city.

So novel was the idea that the Common Council hesitated
for three months before taking action. Even then their opinion
was divided, but the majority voted 8 to 2 to try the experiment.

Even after this action the Common Council was still wary
about the project. When Van Cortlandt offered to sell the site
selected for the reservoir at £600 per acre, the Council went
personally to the property to taste the water. They finally concluded "the same to be a very good quality," then accepted
the offer for the land and notified Colles to proceed.

In August 1774 the Common Council set up a committee
of eight to supervise the construction of the first water works
for the city. A contract was made in Saratoga County for
60,000 linear feet of pitch or yellow pine timber for pipes.
The logs were to be from 14 to 20 feet long, one-fourth of
them to be 12 inches in diameter at the smaller end, three-
fourths to be 9 inches in diameter and all to be "straight and
free from shakes and large knots." Delivery was to be completed by October 1, 1775, at a price of £1250.

While waiting for the timber, Colles proceeded with the
construction of his wells, the reservoir and pumphouse. The
reservoir was planned for a capacity of 20,000 hogsheads;
the well was to be 30 feet in diameter, and the engine to pump
200 gallons per minute 52 feet high. The work as it proceeded
was evidently done in a very durable manner. Old records
show that the roof of the pumphouse was built of curved tiles
so laid that one would have the convex side upward and the
next the concave. Bills were also paid for iron and brazier
work.

An issue of notes amounting to £2600 was voted, later
increased to £9100. These notes were about 2⅓ by 4 inches
in size, and bore the following inscription on the face:

NEW YORK WATER WORKS

(*No............*)

This Note shall entitle the bearer to the sum of

FOUR SHILLINGS

current money of the Colony of New York, payable on Demand, by the Mayor, Aldermen and Commonalty of the City of New York, at the office of the Chamberlain of the said City, pursuant to a Vote of the said Mayor, Aldermen and Commonalty of this Date.

Dated the Sixth Day of January, in the Year of Our Lord One Thousand Seven Hundred and Seventy Six.

By order of the Corporation.

N. Bayard

J. H. Cruger

A picture of a steam pumping engine and two fountains were found on the reverse side.

Unfortunately the Revolutionary War began while the waterworks were still in process of construction. The construction continued until 1776, when it was stopped by the war and never resumed. The British occupied the city, Colles and his family fled, and in time the waterworks became a ruin. After the war Colles returned to New York and presented a petition for the amount due him. This petition is dated October 27, 1784, and reads:

> *To the Honorable Mayor, Aldermen and Common Council of the City of New York.*
>
> *The Humble Memorial of Christopher Colles of said City Engineer Sheweth:*
>
> That your Memorialist in the year 1774 presented a proposal to this honorable corporation for erecting works for supplying this city with water for the sum of eighteen thousand pounds. That this honorable board after sufficient inquiry concerning the practicability of the design Resolved to agree with the said proposal and directed your memorialist to proceed in the execution of the work.
>
> That your memorialist did accordingly proceed in the

execution of the work and erected a reservoir capable
of containing twenty thousand hogsheads of water; dug,
walled, covered and completely finished a well thirty feet
diameter at the inside, from which he pumped by means
of a steam engine which he also erected, two hundred
gallons of water, fifty-two feet high perpendicular per
minute, into the said reservoir.

That previous to the said resolve of the corporation
your memorialist furnished them with an estimate of the
expense of the different parts of the work, agreeable to
which the part executed amounted to the sum of three
thousand six hundred pounds.

That the several sums advanced for the prosecution of
the work amounted to three thousand pounds, conse-
quently, that there remains a balance of six hundred
pounds, one hundred and fifty pounds of which is due
to different artificers for work and the remaining four
hundred and fifty pounds is due said Colles.

That your memorialist in common with other citizens,
friends of society and the interests of mankind, suffered
the most poignant afflictions during the late war, and
with the utmost difficulty procured the common neces-
saries for his family; and being now returned to the city,
where he hopes to devote the remainder of his days in
promoting the welfare of the city and country, he prays
the corporation to use their endeavors to pay him the
balance above referred to, by which he may be enabled
to support his numerous family in credit, and in some
degree of comfort.

May it therefore please your honors, to take the premises into consideration, and grant him that justice and
assistance, which to your judgment shall seem meet.

Christopher Colles

No action was taken at the time, and in 1785 another re-
quest was presented to the Board, Mr. Colles stating "his
desires are of such a poignant nature as to compel him to re-
quest some (though small) yet present assistance." The Council voted him £100 on account in August 1785, and in
November, after another appeal, he was granted an additional
£50. In 1788 he accepted another £50 in full settlement.

The city continued to worry about the water supply, which
would have been in a very bad way except for the help of the
natural supply offered by the fresh-water lake and the Teawater Spring.

In 1799 a group headed by Aaron Burr applied for a charter for the purpose of "supplying the City of New York with
pure and wholesome water." The charter was granted April
2, 1799, incorporating the Manhattan Company, with a capital of $2,000,000. This charter permitted the company to
employ its surplus capital in financial transactions, giving it
a permanent charter in the banking business. Alexander
Hamilton had organized the first banking organization in
New York in 1784, the Bank of New York, which received
its charter in 1792. This bank and a branch of the Bank of
the United States were the only ones in the City of New York
until the Manhattan Company was organized.

Many discussions arose as to whether water or banking was
the real purpose behind the organization of the Manhattan
Company. The company proceeded with plans for a water
system and went into the banking business also.

A reservoir was built on Chambers Street and a distributing
system of wooden pipes was laid. Wells were sunk in the basin
around the fresh-water lake. In 1836 the system was extended
along Broadway as far as Bleecker Street, at which time the
company was supplying about 2,000 homes through about
25 miles of wooden pipe that carried 700,000 gallons a day.

But as the city expanded northward it became apparent
that more water was needed than could be obtained from
wells sunk in the fresh-water lake section. There was continual
talk of a larger supply, and general agreement that it would
have to come from the mainland rather than from the island
of Manhattan itself. As early as 1819 a suggestion was made
to bring water from Rye Pond in Westchester County to a
reservoir at Harlem River, from which it would be distributed
throughout the city. In 1821 a survey was made exploring the
possibility of the Bronx River as a source of supply. Another

proposed plan was to bring water from the Housatonic River by means of a canal. In 1827 the New York Well Company was organized to attempt to obtain water from artesian wells, but the plan was abandoned. A number of other projects were discussed of which nothing came.

CHAPTER XX

Water Comes

In 1830 it was proposed to bring water from the Croton River in Westchester County to New York by means of an open aqueduct or canal. Finally, in 1835, the city by a vote of 17,300 to 5,963 decided to issue $2,500,000 of "water stock" and to proceed with the Croton project.

The proposed open canals were considered cheaper to build, but it was apparent that they were not the solution to a good water supply. After many discussions, a plan for an aqueduct was approved. The aqueduct had many advantages over local water supplies. It made possible taking water from a higher altitude and delivering it at such pressures that pumping would be unnecessary. Water supplied by an aqueduct could also be controlled and distributed more efficiently than when the supply was derived from a number of sources.

The necessary property on the Croton River was acquired and a dam placed across it. The first dam impounded water for a reservoir five miles long, covering about 400 acres. The masonary aqueduct, begun in 1837, passed through the villages of Sing Sing, Tarrytown, Dobbs Ferry, Hastings and Yonkers to the Harlem River opposite 144th Street.

At this point the famous High Bridge was built over which to carry the pipes of the aqueduct. The distance from the source of the water to the High Bridge was 32.88 miles, the bridge itself being 1450 feet long. Two iron pipes, each 36 inches in diameter, were laid over this bridge, and when the capacity had to be increased in 1860 a third pipe 90 inches in diameter was added.

From High Bridge the Croton Aqueduct continued along Tenth Avenue to the Yorkville reservoir, which had a storage capacity of about 150 million gallons. From the Yorkville reservoir a double line of 36-inch iron pipes was laid to Fifth Avenue, and thence down to the reservoir built between 40th and 42nd Streets.

This reservoir was designed to hold 36 feet of water and had a capacity of 20 million gallons. It was opened in 1842 and at that time was described as being "at Murray Hill, a short drive from the city." The total length of the aqueduct from Croton Dam to Fifth Avenue and 42nd Street was 45.562 miles. In 1899 this reservoir was removed to make room for the present Public Library. The Croton water supply finally reached the Worth Street area in 1842.

The Water Board in 1852 secured the land for the reservoir now in Central Park because with a growing population the city was short of storage capacity. About this same time Central Park itself was created, and the reservoir, covering 96 acres, with a capacity of 1,030 million gallons, was included in this area. The new reservoir in Central Park was named Manahatta Lake and is so listed on a map of 1859. The Mayor at the ceremonies opening this new reservoir said, "Our new lake of the Manahatta will far surpass the dimensions of the old Koolch." (Fresh Water Pond)

The city continued its phenomenal growth, and it soon became necessary to consider additional water supplies and additional reservoirs. Another aqueduct was built from the Croton River in 1885-1893. It was built as a tunnel from Croton Lake to a gatehouse at 135th Street and Convent Avenue, a distance of 31 miles, at which point the old and new aqueducts were connected. The old aqueduct at that time was carrying 90 million gallons a day, and the new, 300 million. This was augmented by 22 million gallons a day brought by conduit from the Bronx and Byram Rivers. Finally a much larger dam was built on the Croton which in 1906 began the storage of water to supply a reservoir 19 miles long, with a capacity of 33,800 million gallons.

In the meantime various steps were taken for the construction of smaller reservoirs in various sections of the city, and in the Bronx, Queens and Brooklyn, where local water supplies were being used. The consolidation of Greater New York in 1898, with a population of 3,500,000, created a new water problem. Committees were set up and organizations formed to find a solution. It was decided to go to the Catskill Mountains for an additional supply. This meant the construction of great reservoirs in the mountains to collect the water and the building of a great tunnel beneath the Hudson to bring it to the city.

The Catskill aqueduct, when finally completed, had an interior 17 feet six inches wide and 17 feet high. It was made of concrete of various thicknesses, from one foot at the top and bottom to five feet at the bottom of the arch. Beginning at the city line, pressure tunnels were built. These were of concrete, generally 15 feet in diameter, gradually reduced to 11 feet as they went southward.

The Catskill tunnel was built under the Hudson to the Kensico Reservoir near White Plains in Westchester County. This reservoir is four miles long and stores 38,000 million gallons. From here the aqueduct passes south for 16 miles to Hillview Reservoir in Yonkers near the city line. This reservoir is 36 feet deep, with a capacity of 900 million gallons. In case of emergency this reservoir could be cut out of the system and the water fed directly to the mains under New York City. From the Hillview Reservoir the aqueduct runs five and three-quarter miles to the Harlem River, passes 250 feet below the surface, and then passes through Manhattan Island at depths varying from 218 to 750 feet.

At Clinton and South Streets, Manhattan, the aqueduct crosses under the East River to Brooklyn, and from there it also feeds Queens and Richmond, crossing under the Narrows to reach the latter borough.

In lower New York the Catskill water will rise by gravity to a height of 280 feet above tidewater—the height of a sixteen-story building.

But the water problem of Manhattan became the problem of the Greater New York with its continued growth, and again the cry went up for more water. More reservoirs were built in the Catskills and work was begun on an aqueduct to solve the problem for years to come.

The great Delaware System was put into operation in 1942, the aqueduct being 19½ feet in diameter, with a capacity of 1,800 million gallons a day. It was built from 300 to 600 feet underground as a concrete-lined tunnel through solid rock from the Catskills to Hillview. This aqueduct alone can today supply more water than the entire city uses in a day. When the old Croton, new Croton, Catskill, Bronx River and Delaware aqueducts are all included, they have a capacity of 3,000 million gallons a day. Now the problem is that of enough reservoirs—and enough water to fill them.

In the face of all these precautions, as recently as 1950 the reservoirs fell below the danger point due to lack of rain and snow, and the city found itself facing a water shortage. Individual firms began to dig wells in the basements of their buildings to secure water for the operation of their new air-cooling systems. Again the surface of Manhattan was being punctured with holes in search of water. At the depth of seventy feet, water was secured on Worth Street between Broadway and Church, but it was brackish just as it was three hundred years ago.

New York's problem of an adequate water supply for its millions is unique. It could not meet the demand if every drop of water that fell upon its surface as rain or snow could be caught, stored and utilized. The average rainfall for the city is 44.63 inches per year, and this, in terms of water, would be about 200,000 million gallons, an average of about 600 million gallons a day. At present the consumption in the city as a whole is over one billion gallons a day. Aqueducts and reservoirs will not solve the basic problem unless there is ample rain and snow to keep them filled. Man is feeble in the face of nature and its inexorable laws.

The original inhabitants of Manhattan, the Manhattes, showed their appreciation for the ample supply of clear fresh water from the lake and springs with a rain dance ceremony. They suffered no shortages of water. But now, even with an elaborate system of aqueducts and reservoirs in the Catskills, New Yorkers still find themselves dependent upon the same basic source of supply of water as did the Manhattes—the rain and snow, over which they have little or no control.

Chapter XXI

The Romance of Textiles

The romance of textiles begins with the story of man himself. Skill in weaving fibers was one of the chief advances toward a civilized state as that term is generally applied. Once man learned to weave fabrics for clothing he was no longer dependent upon skins of animals to cover his body, and he was started on his upward path. And as he went forward through the ages, textiles played an important part in his daily living, his affairs and the affairs of nations.

Worth Street and textiles are today so interwoven that the mention of one immediately brings up the thought of the other. While Worth Street as the primary textile market of the world goes back only a century, it has behind it a textile heritage of thousands of years.

It is a far cry from the busy Worth Street of today, where the products of hundreds of modern mills are handled, to Biblical times, yet there is a direct connection, an unbroken story that has come down through the centuries.

There is something fundamental about textiles. It is not difficult to produce a thread or yarn from a natural fiber such as wool or cotton. The fiber can be taken into one hand and drawn out by the thumb and forefinger of the other, maintaining a twisting motion as the operation proceeds. The stretching and twisting, if done slowly and evenly, will produce a long, continuous thread. These threads may then be woven into fabrics. For thousands of years yarns were hand-spun and fabrics hand-woven.

Flax, cotton, silk and wool are the best-known natural fibers.

90

The manufacture of fine linen fabrics was an established industry in the valley of the Nile. Ireland was exporting linen as early as the thirteenth century. Cotton was being grown and spun in Egypt in 3000 B.C., and the manufacture of cotton fabric was well established in India before the time of Alexander.

Wool was being spun and woven into fabrics before the beginning of written history. While still living in caves man domesticated the sheep to provide a source of food and clothing. When Abraham went up out of Egypt he drove his flocks before him. Wool weaving was introduced to the English by the Romans in 80 A.D., and the English looms soon gained a world-wide reputation.

Silk was first obtained from the cocoon of the silkworm in China some 6,000 years ago, and silk culture became a major industry under Emperor Huang-ti as long ago as 2640 B.C. So important was this industry that the ancient silk caravan route connecting China with the Middle East and Europe became a main artery of trade and held this position for over four thousand years.

Spinning and weaving were for many years household industries. The textile needs of each family were limited and it was possible to meet these in the home—producing the fiber, spinning the yarn and weaving the fabric. In the sixteenth and seventeenth centuries there was a marked increase in the demand for fabrics, and manufacturing plants arose. The textile industry was well established in the Old World when the New World was discovered.

The Indians who originally inhabited Manhattan had learned to twist fibers into fishing lines long before the coming of the white man. According to legend they grew a fiber which they spun and wove into fabric. Whether this was a grass or some form of cotton is not known.

A knowledge of flax-growing and the weaving of linen was brought to America by the earliest settlers and flourished until the invention of the cotton gin in 1793, when cotton became

the pre-eminent vegetable fiber. Silk culture was introduced
by King James I at an early date, but the venture was unsuc-
cessful. It was not long until cotton was introduced in Virginia
and the Carolinas; however, for some time England continued
to obtain its supply from the Barbadoes, the West Indies,
Brazil and India. The English brought the first flock of sheep
to Jamestown, Virginia, in 1609.

The Dutch in the small settlement around Fort Amsterdam
spun and wove fibers into fabrics for their personal family
use, and this custom persisted into the English era. During
these two eras, however, the major textile needs of the ever-
growing population were largely met by imports. This was
especially true among the more prosperous. The attractive
foreign fabrics naturally had a greater appeal than the crude
homespuns. Furthermore, the settlers in Manhattan were
traders rather than husbandmen, and textiles were an item of
trade. The importation of textiles soon became a business of
consequence and many men engaged in it.

The first American effort toward mill production of textiles
was in 1638, when Ezekiel Rogers, founder of the town of
Rowley, Massachusetts, built a small fulling mill. He and his
associates have been described as "the first people that set
upon making cloth in this western world." Cotton from the
Barbadoes was used, as well as imported flax and hemp, but
today there are no records of the mill's operation. This early
mill was a more or less isolated case, and the American textile
industry did not really start until after the Revolution. As a
matter of fact, textiles may be regarded as one of the indirect
causes of the separation of the Colonies from England.

The manufacture of textiles in mills was a major industry
in England in the second half of the eighteenth century, and
more and more people were becoming dependent upon this
industry for their livelihood. The prosperity of the country
was deeply involved in finding markets overseas for the output of these mills. It was never the policy of England to foster
and encourage manufacture in the Colonies, since they were

looked upon as rich markets for exports. Many in England believed that the purpose of the Colonies was to absorb the manufactured goods of the mother country.

About this time several inventions greatly increased the output of the English mills. In 1770, James Hargreaves patented a spinning jenny—an invention which made it possible to spin twenty or thirty threads with no more labor than was previously required to spin one. This device had evidently been in use several years before it was patented. Richard Arkwright, who was born in 1732 and died in 1792, improved on Hargreaves' invention and may be regarded as the father of the modern textile mill. In 1768 Dr. Edmund Cartwright invented a power loom. So jealous was England of its textile industry that workmen familiar with these new inventions were not permitted to emigrate to the Colonies.

In the decade prior to the Revolution there was cotton manufacturing going on, in a small way, in the Cheraw settlement of South Carolina. The mill was started in 1768, and by the next year people were buying cotton goods at the mill and there was a movement to stimulate cotton manufacture further in the Colony. Writing to his son in 1777, Daniel Hayward made the following statement: "My manufacturing goes on bravely, but want of cards will put a stop to it because they cannot be got. If they were, there would be the least doubt that we would make 6000 yards of cloth in the year." This was a small mill serving the people living near it. It may safely be said that at the beginning of the Revolution the Colonies had very few textile mills, and that aside from the cloth produced in homes the Colonists were dependent upon England for their needs.

Open rebellion against the British Crown was responsible for the first effort at large-scale textile production in Manhattan. The Patriots Society was organized in 1760 to oppose the British and carry out economic sanctions against them. In 1770 the members of the Society, urged on by the "Daughters of the Patriots," decided to produce collectively all the yarn and fabrics required by members of the New York Colony and thus obviate the need for imported goods.

They succeeded to a surprising degree. Each home kept the spinning wheel and hand loom going into the night. For the first time individuals were producing more than they needed for themselves and their households, and the surplus was bartered for commodities or labor when it could not be sold for cash. Despite these valiant efforts, the Colony suffered a shortage of fabrics for clothing its army when the British blockade cut off imported goods. The goods that did get through the blockade consisted largely of duck for sails and fabrics urgently needed by the army. It soon became apparent that people working in their homes could not meet the demand for textiles, and that America needed a textile mill industry of its own.

Chapter XXII

Pioneering in Production

Once the Revolution was over, the legislatures of the various states turned their attention to encouraging textile production. In 1786 the Massachusetts Legislature secured some models of Arkwright's improved textile machinery, and in the same year members of the House and Senate were appointed to inspect any new textile machinery that might be developed. The first venture of this committee was to inspect some machines made by Alexander and Robert Barr, two brothers from Scotland. The legislature contributed £200 to assist them in completing these machines. The experiment failed, and the machines were sent to Providence to Moses Brown. Later they were condemned as unsatisfactory.

Thomas Somers, an Englishman, in 1786 returned to his native country where he secured descriptions of models of machines and brought these to Baltimore, where he attempted to interest the merchants of that city to help him set up a mill, but he failed. He then appealed to the Massachusetts Legislature, which granted him £20 as "encouragement." A building was erected in Beverly, Massachusetts, in the fall of 1787, but there is some difference of opinion as to when operations really began. The power for this small mill was furnished by two horses turning a wheel.

The mill was known as the Beverly Manufacturing Company and was equipped with nine jennies, one doubling and twisting machine, one slubbing machine, one warping machine, sixteen looms with flying shuttles, and some dyeing equipment. It produced about 10,000 yards of cloth a year, all of which was sold locally. This was an average production of 600 yards per year per loom; today, a coarse-fabric loom will produce that much in less than a week.

Corduroys, bed ticking, cotton velvets, jeans, shirtings, sheeting and tablecloths were produced—an assortment much larger than any individual mill would attempt today. George Washington mentioned this enterprising little establishment in his diary under date of October 30, 1789. The mill prospered and continued in operation for about forty years—until it was destroyed by fire, in 1828. Brief records tell of another New England mill, the Boston Sail Cloth Manufactory, which was in operation between 1788 and 1796, but not much is now known about it.

In Pennsylvania the Society for the Encouragement of Manufactures and Fine Arts was organized in 1787. The first textile mill built under this program was the United Company of Philadelphia, which produced linen yarn. An experimental loom was added in 1788, and soon the plant had 28 looms making corduroys, beavers, jeans and plain cottons. This mill also burned down, in 1790.

The encouragement of manufacturing was more a matter of state participation than a national program. The New York Manufacturing Society opened a mill in 1789 with a carding machine and two jennies, employing 130 spinners and 14 weavers. There were also small manufactories for making duck at Worcester and Haverhill, in Massachusetts.

A small mill was set up on the Santee River near Statesburg, South Carolina, in 1789, and there was also one near Charleston. There are some reports of a mill located at Norwich, Connecticut, 1790, but details are lacking.

These were all small crude plants set up in frame buildings, hardly deserving the name of factory or mill, but they were the beginnings of what was to become a great industry.

The textile industry in the United States received a great impetus when a young man named Samuel Slater landed in New York in 1788. Born in England in 1768, Slater became an expert machinist in the first mill to be completely equipped with Richard Arkwright's newly invented waterpower system of cotton processing. Although the law expressly forbade machinists to leave England, Slater managed to emigrate to America, bringing an accurate and expert knowledge of the cotton spinning jenny and other textile machines.

Within a few months after Slater's arrival, with his help Moses Brown built a mill in Providence which began operation December 20, 1790. This plant was owned by the firm of Almy, Brown and Slater, and consisted of three cards, drawing and roving, two spinning frames of 72 spindles each, and a water wheel. Slater was able to reproduce from memory the Arkwright machinery. The Slater machines were handmade, with wooden frames. Crude in construction, they nevertheless made possible the building of comparatively larger textile mills in America. A later mill building, still standing, was constructed by the Slater interests in 1793.

An American invention of 1793 was destined to revolutionize the cotton industry. In that year Eli Whitney built the first cotton gin—a device that could separate the cotton lint from the seed by mechanical means. Until then the separation of the cotton fiber from the seed had been a costly and tedious process. As a matter of fact, until this time comparatively little cotton had been raised in the United States. Now that there was a way to gin the raw fiber, cotton could be made ready in quantity for processing by the mills, Southern economy shifted over to cotton-raising on a large scale.

Other textile mills were built, such as that of the Wilkinson Brothers, who in 1793 started a factory for twisting yarn into sewing thread. This innovation is supposed to have followed an idea of Hannah Wilkinson Slater, the wife of Samuel Slater. One of the earlier plants was the Eastchester Manufacturing Company, in Yonkers, New York, whose operations were carried on in an old stone building, still standing, which was erected between 1805 and 1810. It is situated on the Bronx River near the Tuckahoe Railroad Station.

The growth of the textile industry in the early years of the United States was not spectacular, but it was steady and healthy. In 1808 there were reports of 15 mills with a total of 8000 spindles in operation, while in 1809 there were 87 small mills with a total of 31,000 spindles, or an average of about 350 spindles per mill. The census of cotton mills by states in 1810 showed that Connecticut had 14 mills, Delaware 3, Kentucky 15, Maryland 11, Massachusetts 54, New Jersey 4, New York 26, Ohio 2, Pennsylvania 64, Rhode Island 28, Tennessee 4 and Vermont one.

These small mills scattered about the country reflected the ambition of many individuals to get into the business of making fabrics. They were beset, however, with many difficulties in trying to secure machinery, and faced even greater problems in securing maintenance parts needed to keep it in operation. Power was also a factor, since the only cheap power then available was obtained from water wheels. For that reason the early mills were all built upon streams. This was one reason for the wide geographical distribution of the mills.

Transportation was another problem. The mills had to be built where water power was available, and this was usually far from the large concentrated markets of cities. The result was that mills were at first forced to dispose of their products locally. On the other hand, the products of these early mills were usually well adapted for use in rural homes—sturdy fabrics from which plain clothing might be made. They were not yet the fine products found in imported goods that appealed to the well-to-do city dwellers.

The invention of the cotton gin also changed the balance of fibers used for the manufacture of textiles. Before this invention, cotton fabric was a luxury item with a limited demand. It has been estimated that in the 1780's about 75 per cent of American textile consumption was in woolen goods, while linen was second with 18 per cent and cotton represented only

4 per cent. This picture was rapidly revised when raw cotton became available in large quantities.

After the Revolution, despite the fact that the American textile industry was getting started in more or less isolated little mills scattered about the country, the demands in the larger cities and those having port facilities were largely met by imports. Since Manhattan had no great natural sources of water power, it soon became apparent that it would not be a great textile manufacturing center. But the excellent harbor made importing attractive.

The War of 1812, with its blockades and embargoes, again cut off imports from foreign shores, especially England, at that time the greatest textile nation. The young United States was forced once more to fill its wants from domestic goods. New cotton mills were built. By 1816 the cotton industry had expanded to 500,000 spindles, with an invested capital of $50,000,000, and the mills were employing 100,000 workers.

The first successful mill in the South was probably the Lincoln Cotton Factory, established in 1813 at Lexington, North Carolina. The handmade machines came from Rhode Island, and the mill continued to operate until it was burned during the War Between the States. In the same year the Waltham Company in Massachusetts began operations under the ownership of Francis Cabot Lowell and associates, with 3000 spindles and power looms that produced 4000 yards a week.

The Rocky Mount Mill, still in operation, was built at Rocky Mount, North Carolina, in 1818. The Merrimack Manufacturing Company was built at Lowell, Massachusetts, in 1823, and in 1835 one of the first steam railroads in America was built to serve this, and other, mills in the vicinity. The Graniteville Manufacturing Company, in Graniteville, South Carolina, also still in operation, was built in 1845.

With the great expansion in the field of domestic mills, marketing and distribution became a problem. At first, as we have seen, the products of mills were sold locally for cash;

when the local cash market was taken care of, small mills sent their surplus stocks to merchants in near-by towns on consignment. This was not too satisfactory. In time, wholesalers of other products added textiles to their lines, and their salesmen peddled the products on a commission basis. These salesmen went up and down the coast and as far west as the new states of Kentucky and Ohio. There were no well-organized methods of marketing and distribution, and each mill was more or less on its own.

Chapter XXIII

The Beginning of Worth Street

After the War of 1812, imports again began to arrive, and it is not surprising that for a while the markets in cities were again dominated by foreign goods. In New York importers congregated near the docks where the sailing ships arrived with merchandise. Auction sales held every two weeks in certain seasons of the year started much of the imported material into distribution. British, French and German mills advertised textiles for sale by lots and packages.

But while this was going on, the enterprising American mills were finding ways to expand their markets too. They gradually widened their fields, carrying the goods to markets first by wagon and then by means of the many little railroads which were springing up around the country. In this way the domestic goods reached cities like Boston, Philadelphia and Baltimore. When these city markets became oversold, goods were placed on boats and sent to New York. Importing firms in New York began selling both foreign and domestic goods, and soon a thriving business was built up with the American mills.

New York merchant houses were of various origins. Some were importers of textiles who added domestic fabrics; others began as general merchants; still others began as ship chandlers handling anchors, chains, sails, cordage and tarpaulins. Most of these houses, from the beginning, combined financial operations with merchandising as a matter of necessity, and this had a distinct influence upon the development of many Worth Street firms of today.

101

The textile merchants of New York were well established in lower Pearl Street when the great fire of 1835 scattered them overnight. These merchants were already an important factor in the domestic textile industry, since the mills were now depending upon them for outlets, and in many cases for financing. The textile merchants soon realized that they must again concentrate in one center.

In 1850 the entire production of cotton goods by American mills amounted to about $60,000,000 while the importation of foreign textiles into the port of New York for the year amounted to the same sum. In short, New York was importing and distributing foreign goods equal in value to the total production of American cotton mills. New York then probably ranked fourth in handling the American goods, Boston, Philadelphia and Baltimore all doing more business in domestic textiles because of their proximity to the mills. (This picture was to change greatly during the next century, when the concentrated market in New York would become of great importance as the population mushroomed.) It was during this decade that the textile merchants began to move to the Worth Street area.

From 1850 to 1853 a number of dry goods firms, importers, wholesalers and retailers moved into the Worth Street area. In 1850 the dry goods firm of Hitchcock and Leadbeater was doing both a wholesale and a retail business at 347 Broadway, corner of Leonard Street; Peter Roberts, at 375 Broadway, was an importer of embroidery and laces; Thomas Shepherd was at 371 Broadway, and A. & M. Viel at 47 Lispenard Street. Seaman and Muir opened as dry goods wholesalers and importers in 1851 at 321 Broadway, corner of Thomas Street. By 1853 a dozen importing and wholesale houses were centered in the Worth Street area, which by then was recognized as the wholesale center. Textile merchants were seeking permanent business locations, and changing conditions in the Worth Street area made it possible for them to purchase properties and build their own buildings to suit themselves. The Broadway Tabernacle had an entrance at 340 Broadway, with its building to the rear extending from 95 to 103 Worth Street. John Phelps bought the Tabernacle property in 1857, and a year later sold it to George Bliss & Co., the predecessor of the present-day firm of James H. Dunham & Co. The Bliss Company in 1858 also bought the Broadway frontage—numbers 340 to 344—and erected a handsome stone-front building. The establishment of this firm in its own fine building settled the question of the neighborhood's future as the great textile center. In 1861 Claflin, Mellen & Co. erected what was then regarded as an enormous commercial building covering the block now known as 40 Worth Street.

Houses in other cities began opening branch offices in Manhattan, since the New York market's potentials were becoming more and more apparent. Francis Skinner & Co. of Boston opened a branch at 2 College Place (West Broadway and Barclay Streets) in 1846. This firm was a selling agency. The move was strongly protested by other Boston firms, and when a committee was set up in that city to study the matter it reported that they had "been bred to believe that a seller should keep his goods at home, and allow the purchaser to come to him." This bold move on the part of the Skinner firm in "going to the purchaser" was a milestone in textile distribution. The move was followed by more out-of-town firms. Parker Wilder & Co., also of Boston, opened a Worth Street area branch in 1861, and two years later Woodward, Baldwin & Co., of Baltimore, opened an office in Duane Street. From this time forward Worth Street crystallized as the primary mill-agency market in the United States.

The years preceding the War Between the States were ones of great activity. The nation was rapidly expanding, and this expansion created a greater need for textiles. Railroads had been built, and were being built, and transportation was no longer the problem it had been. More and more mills were being built to meet the growing needs of the people. Laboring men called for more and more sturdy goods for clothing and for use in their homes.

The English mills, depending to a great extent upon the cotton raised in the South of the United States, had become very efficient and were in keen competition with the fast-growing American mills. The War Between the States changed this picture considerably. As the war progressed, the South was cut off as a source of supply for cotton for the English mills. The North found itself largely dependent upon American mills for textiles, and the great military demands were added to normal requirements. Great merchants arose in the Worth Street area—men who took it upon themselves to meet the responsibility of supplying textiles to meet both civilian and military needs.

The end of the war saw the American textile industry firmly established and looking forward to a new and greater era of expansion. When the hospital was torn down in 1870 and new buildings were erected on its site, such textile firms as were still located below Chambers Street moved into the village to occupy these buildings. "Worth Street" began as a wholesale textile market place in 1853, became established as the primary-mill agency market in 1861 and was recognized as the textile center in 1870.

In the latter part of the nineteenth century and early part of the twentieth, Worth Street and its environs were also the market place for many other products, such as carpets, clothing, corsets and even furs. Gradually these other merchants moved to other parts of the city, since it was impossible for them to secure room for expansion in Worth Village.

The business of Worth Street today is based upon the products of all textile fibers: cotton, the sunshine fiber; wool, the animal fiber; and rayon and the other synthetic fibers. Man-made fibers had their commercial beginnings after World War I, and came into their own during World War II. Today great plants are producing rayon, Nylon, and a variety of others, such as Orlon, Dacron and Dynel. All textile fibers, whatever their origin, have their place in Worth Street.

Eight-tenths of Worth Street's business now is based on cotton. The statistics regarding the immense cotton crop of the United States are fascinating. In 1951 cotton was grown on more than 29,500,000 acres across the southern part of the nation. This great crop required the growing of more than 700,000,000,000 stalks, each stalk being a beautifully formed "tree" from two to five feet tall. The ancients regarded cotton as a type of wool growing on trees. (The German name for cotton—*baumwolle*—carries out this thought.) They pictured lambs growing on small trees, each in a downy pod. These lambs were supposed to lean from the stems to graze until all the grass in their orbits was consumed; then the expiring lambs were supposed to yield their "cotton wool."

The sunshine fiber is made from sunshine, water and the good earth. As it nestles and is nourished in the small bolls, the sunshine gives it radiance, the rain elasticity, the cool nights toughness, and the morning dew its glossy finish. It is not surprising that cotton makes such fine sunshine clothing and the best rainwear known, that it washes so well—water being its second nature—and that it dries so perfectly in the sun. Its fibers are tough and strong by nature, and when entwined together in yarns and fabrics make an ideal product for the sheerest of garments or for the roughest of uses—for work or play.

In addition to its strength and elasticity, nature has endowed the cotton fiber with essential curves and convolutions. This spirality and curl make it readily adaptable for manufacturing processes and for a wide number of uses. The tiny fiber itself has a hollow core running down its center.

The statistics of cotton production, when expressed in pounds, show the vast importance of the role this fiber plays. About one hundred million cotton fibers of the usual average staple variety are required to make a pound of cotton. This means that the average cotton dress contains approximately that number of fibers, while a woman in a fashionable cotton outfit utilizing many yards of cloth might find herself wrapped in three hundred million fibers. A man's shirt may contain from fifty to a hundred million cotton fibers, depending upon the fabric and yardage used. A man dressed completely in cotton may be wearing as many as five hundred million cotton fibers. An 81-by-108-inch bed sheet, a heavy bath towel, a pair of overalls, would each contain one hundred million fibers.

Every year some twenty to forty pounds of cotton are used in the United States to supply the needs of each American. Some uses are readily apparent, as in the case of clothing and household goods; some are less obvious, being concealed in automobiles, tires, wire covering and thousands of other industrial uses. In 1950 the figure was 30.7 pounds per person, which, multiplied by one hundred million fibers to the pound, means 3,070 million of these fibers for each man, woman and child in this country. When it is taken into consideration that every household has a large inventory of cotton items, it is only necessary to add them up to find that there are at least 200 pounds of cotton in every home. Translated into fibers, this gives the great sum of twenty thousand million.

The annual cotton crop of some 16 million bales, each weighing 500 pounds, would form an immense pile greater by ten times than the greatest Egyptian pyramid. The cotton textile industry annually weaves about 11,000 million square yards of cloth. If this were all in 80-square print cloth, 36 inches wide, the industry would have to spin 2,280,960,000,000,000 inches of yarn (thread) to produce it. The great part of the 800,000,000,000,000,000,000 fibers in the annual cotton crop, turned into 2,280,960,000,000,000 inches of yarn, and then woven into 11,000,000,000 yards of cloth, finds a market through Worth Street channels, along with a substantial portion of the 2,500,000,000 yards of rayon and other man-made fabrics.

The story of Worth Village as the textile center of the world is really the story of the great American textile industry itself, since one cannot be divorced from the other. The history of Worth Street is part of the history of the mills, and the history of the mills is part of the history of Worth Street. Some sixty firms in Worth Village today handle the output of the larger part of the cotton mills of the nation.

The growth of the American textile industry was to a large extent made possible through the development of the primary-mill market in Worth Street. In the period between 1860 and 1890 the mills came to depend upon this market not only for orders but in some instances for financing of sales and production. It was a critical period in the building up of a great industry. How well the plan worked is reflected by the size of the industry today. What sort of men made this possible? The mill men were pioneers in the field of production, and the textile merchants were a sturdy lot. Both were dedicated to the task of building up a great industry. A few still remember some of these early mill men and merchants and their methods of doing business in an era of keenest competition. And there are those who still remember some of the old offices.

There was a discipline in Worth Street, with careful economies and close supervision of details. The merchant located himself where he could watch every activity of his subordinates, including the bookkeepers on tall stools. The early stores were arranged strictly for utility and business. When the telephone came, the average merchant would not tolerate the innovation. Calls were made and received for him, but he would not touch the instrument himself. Even the typewriter was slow in arriving, and statements were written in longhand. For many years only men were employed in the offices as clerks, and it almost took a revolution in later years to admit women as stenographers.

These early years were years of distinguished dress, when the merchant adopted the plug hat and the frock coat of the best broadcloth as a virtual uniform that set him apart from others and contributed in no small measure to his prestige and business success.

The economies practiced by many of these merchants in building up their businesses are amusing by today's standards. The motto of these offices was "work and more work." There was one early merchant who lived in Brooklyn and drove to his Worth Village office each day in a one-horse buggy. Upon his arrival the horse was taken out of the buggy shafts and the vehicle parked on West Broadway. Then the horse was saddled and used to deliver packages, invoices and messages. At six each evening the horse was unsaddled, hitched to the buggy again, and the merchant drove home.

Another early merchant arrived at his office at six-thirty each morning. Since it was usually dark, especially in winter, he brought his dog with him for companionship and protection. As each employee arrived, the dog would rush forward to greet him and then follow him to his desk. If an employee was late, the dog would walk back and forth from the vacant desk to that of his master calling attention to the absence of the employee.

Buying and selling were the life blood of these old merchants. One eminent man with large mills and a great volume of textiles to sell prided himself on the fact that no two buyers were ever given the same price, and that seldom did any one buyer know the price another was paying. A buyer even hesitated to ask another buyer, fearing that he would either disclose his own inside price or permit his competitor to learn he had paid more. This merchant was a trader from morning to night, and his office was a place turbulent with rounds of debates with buyers. Some called this man a brilliant trader, others questioned his methods, but he made progress for himself and his mills in his day.

It took many men to establish Worth Street as the great textile center. Some are remembered and some forgotten, but all contributed something—a certain basic honesty and integrity which still prevails in the market and in the industry.

Chapter XXIV

Some of the Pioneers

Volumes could be written about the firms that have made history in Worth Street, each story an epic of its own centered around men fired with ambition, imagination and an urge to own and produce. Each story is a part of the drama of America, a small business with limited capital, often pioneered by a single individual who placed his all in a venture and backed it with a family name.

Worth Street has been blessed with many such pioneers, fine merchants who organized hundreds of firms, some of which date back to the early 1800's. Some of its founding fathers already are becoming legendary. Perhaps the most celebrated was a great merchant with the curious name of Preserved Fish. Some sources relate that Preserved Fish, whose dignified portrait hangs today in the Chamber of Commerce of the State of New York, was so named because he was found as a baby afloat on a raft in Buzzard's Bay, and was thus preserved from the fish. A story was written in 1946 to refute this legend and to trace his ancestry back beyond the raft, for it seems "Preserved" was not a rare name for a boy with Puritan ancestry.

It seems that a little fish sometimes catches a big one: at the age of twenty-one, Preserved Fish shipped as captain of a whaler out of New England. He soon decided that there were enough people gathering whale oil and not enough creating a market for it, so he gave up the sea to enter upon a sales career. In 1816, one Saul Alley decided to go into business for himself, which he set up under his name. Preserved Fish and one Joseph Lawrence joined him. Hides, leather and whale oil were dealt in originally, but soon some textiles came down Long Island Sound and the firm was in the textile business. While the name of the firm was changed many times, it operated in more recent years as Taylor, Pinkham & Co., until taken over in 1952 by J. P. Stevens & Co., Inc. Preserved Fish lived at a time when the textile houses were near the toe of Manhattan, so he saw the great crossroads of Manhattan only in his idler moments, but he helped set a pattern of mercantile accomplishment for the Worth Street of today.

There was a great family of textile merchants who also began business in the old textile market on lower Manhattan but later moved to Worth Street. Galey & Lord, now a division of Burlington Mills, was established in Worth Street in 1897 by William T. Galey, Charles E. Lord and Kenneth Lord. The Lord family, however, had started in the textile business much earlier. Rufus Lord came to New York about 1805 and became a junior partner in the wholesale firm of Carnes & Lord. Later he founded the firm of Lord and Olmstead, dry goods, at 172 Pearl Street. In 1822 it became the firm of Lord and Lee, which did a large business in imported goods.

A little later his brother Thomas Lord entered the firm, and in 1830 he continued the business under his name. David Lord, another brother, started in the dry goods business about this time. In the interim, Rufus Lord had acquired large realty holdings on Exchange Place and built a beautiful row of stores, one of which was occupied by Edwin Lord & Co. at 52 Exchange Place, another by David Lord at No. 50, and a third by Thomas Lord at No. 46. They were all in the wholesale dry goods business, and the row was nicknamed "Lord's Beautiful Row." The great fire of 1835 destroyed these stores, along with other textile firms, and the store of Edwin Lord was blown up in an attempt to arrest the fire.

Charles Asaph Lord, son of Edwin, went to work for Stone & Co., his uncle's business, at 46 Exchange Place, and after the fire moved to 134 Duane Street. He continued doing business at this same place after the dissolution of Stone & Co. in 1862. In 1863 he was at 18 Park Place, in 1866 at 18 Reade Street, in 1869 at 64 Reade Street, and in 1871 at 47 Walker Street, where the firm name was Lord & DeBeau Bros. He moved to Philadelphia in 1873 and there went into the textile business with William T. Galey, and later with John C. Watt under the name of Economy Textile Co. There by 1889 they were producing the finest gingham made in this country. His oldest son, Charles E. Lord, later joined Galey in forming the Aberfoyle Manufacturing Co., Chester, Pa., with offices at 99 Franklin Street. In 1897 they were joined by Kenneth Lord in the firm of Galey & Lord at 83-85 Worth Street. As stated, the firm now is a part of the great Burlington Mills organization.

Another firm had its start 122 years ago in the old textile center on lower Manhattan and was among the first wholesale houses to settle in Worth Street. In 1831, Amos R. Eno of Hartford, Conn., established on lower Pearl Street the business that is today James H. Dunham & Company. As the business grew, he took as partner John J. Phelps, and as Eno and Phelps they continued at 16 Wall Street. On the retirement of Mr. Eno, who built the famous Fifth Avenue Hotel, and the admission as partners of S. B. Chittenden and George Bliss, the firm became Phelps, Chittenden and Bliss, locating at Broadway and Rector Street. George Bliss later bought the block front on Broadway between Worth Street and Catherine Lane, the former site of the famous "Broadway Tabernacle," which was the location of the establishment from 1858 until 1935. George Bliss retired to enter the banking house of Morton, Bliss and Company in 1868, leaving the business in the hands of Eldredge, Dunham & Co.

James Harvey Dunham was born in Pittsfield, Mass., in 1832. He began his career in the dry goods business in New Haven and joined the firm in 1855. In 1874 Mr. Eldredge retired and Mr. Dunham took William T. Buckley as partner, and the firm was known as Dunham, Buckley & Company, until Mr. Buckley retired in 1898, when it assumed the present name of James H. Dunham & Company. It was incorporated under that name in July 1901, shortly after Mr. Dunham's death, and William A. Little became president. At Mr. Little's death in 1931, John C. McMullen took over the presidency; on his death in December 1947, Robert Jenkins became president.

In its 121 years of operation, the business changed from the early importing phase to the jobbing of innumerable lines, and finally to a modern organization converting and distributing nationally cotton piece goods, house furnishings and allied lines. This firm is one of the original Worth Street houses, with the unique distinction of having been located in the Worth Street market place longer than any other firm.

Few names arouse more memories in Worth Street than that of Horace B. Claflin. This merchant—today he would be called a wholesaler—represented probably the pinnacle in dry goods distribution of his day. He came to New York in 1843 after a business experience in Worcester and Milford, Mass., and formed the firm of Bulkley & Claflin at 46 Cedar Street, which in 1852 became Claflin Mellen & Co. In 1861 the firm moved to Worth Street, to a large new building that covered the entire block bounded by Worth, Church and Thomas Streets and West Broadway, the site of the present building known as 40 Worth Street. In 1864 it became H. B. Claflin & Co. The business prospered, and in one Civil War year ran up the then amazing total of $72,000,000 of sales.

The merchants of Worth Street in 1876 joined in a tribute to Mr. Claflin for his vindication in a malicious charge of customs evasion, an issue now long forgotten. But the tribute is of interest because it reveals the names of some of the leading textile firms of more than three-quarters of a century ago. They included Parker, Wilder & Co.; Wright, Bliss & Fabyan; Woodward, Lawrence & Co.; Denny Poor & Co.; Joy, Langdon & Co.; Lawrence & Co.; Minot Hooper & Co.; J. L.

Bremer & Co.; Fred Butterfield & Co.; Garner & Co.; W. L. Strong & Co., and George C. Richardson & Co. It was a dark day for Worth Street when the great Claflin firm fell in 1914, the year that ushered in World War I and produced probably the severest strain the cotton and textile economy ever experienced. As Claflins, Inc., the business was re-established and continued until its final dissolution in 1926.

Only one block away from the old Claflin site, at 250 Church Street, is the Worth Street office of Ely Walker Dry Goods Company, whose headquarters are in St. Louis, Mo. This firm is the largest wholesale organization in the country today. It has also become an important factor in several types of manufacturing, including large interests in several cotton mills.

An earlier business had been formed by the founders of the firm in 1872, when Frank Ely and David Walker as partners, together with Wayman Crow, William Hargadine and Hugh McKettrick, organized the firm of Crow-McCreery & Co., which was later changed to Crow-Hargadine Co. In 1878 Frank Ely left this firm and formed a partnership with A. A. Janis and Henry Canoll under the name of Ely Janis & Co., with a capital of $75,000. Two years later David Walker joined the company, and the name was changed to Ely Walker & Co. Headquarters were at 512 Locust Street, St. Louis, in a building with a twenty-five-foot frontage. In 1883 the business was incorporated as Ely and Walker Dry Goods Co., and in 1907 moved to its present quarters at 1520 Washington Avenue, St. Louis. In 1930 E. P. Cave became president. The firm's first announcement of business as Ely, Janis & Co., in 1878, contained the following statement: "We shall confine our business to cash, both in buying and selling, as this system will let our goods reach the trade on closer margins than any other."

Thomas Wilson & Co., Inc. moved to 44 White Street in the Worth Street area in 1875, in 1880 to 42 White Street, and in 1889 to 360 Broadway. The business started as a partnership of Robert and George Wilson in 1839 at 102 Liberty

Street, moving in 1850 to 36 Church Street and in 1858 to 62 Church Street. The business has been in continuous operation for 114 years. In 1916 it was incorporated, and is now located at 200 Madison Avenue with Henry Giebel as president.

Worth Street over the years has produced men noted in many fields, among whom might be mentioned a Vice-President of the United States, Levi P. Morton, who served under President Benjamin Harrison from 1889 to 1893, but who in 1843 had organized the firm of Morton & Grinnell before he turned to banking in 1863.

Cornelius N. Bliss was another textile man of broad affairs and widespread public interests, who served as Secretary of the Interior in the cabinet of President McKinley, while W. L. Strong became Mayor of New York. In fact, one will find interesting parallels between leadership in textile market life and political affairs, beginning with signers of the Declaration of Independence, four of whom were "merchants" and at least two or three of whom dealt in textiles, and extending on down to the present day. In more recent years, Myron C. Taylor, the President's personal representative to the Vatican, and Senator Herbert Lehman, both made their mark after leaving the Street. Robert T. Stevens has recently become Secretary of the Army and John C. Hughes, NATO ambassador.

The role that many textile merchants of the past played in building America is often forgotten today. These men had much to do with furnishing the sails—the motive power—for the great clipper ships. At one time there were four hundred of these ships in operation. The *Golden Eagle,* for instance, used about seven thousand yards of canvas for a set of sails, while the *Great Republic,* the largest sailing vessel ever constructed in the United States, used 15,653 yards. Every clipper carried two full sets of sails, of which a portion was lost on every voyage.

This extensive use of duck for sails suddenly ceased about 1855, just as Worth Street was developing as a textile center;

but then the need for duck for prairie-schooner covers took over. Today hatch covers for steamships, tarpaulins for trucks, and hundreds of other modern uses demand more duck than ever.

Chapter XXV

Century-Old Firms

It is unfortunate that so many of the old records of the great firms of Worth Street have disappeared. This is a loss to the industry as a whole, because these records made up an important part of the history of textiles and business in America. From available records, brief biographies of a number of firms have been prepared. The purpose was not so much to show the histories of individual firms as to put their stories together in an attempt to create a more comprehensive story, a better understanding, of the textile industry and Worth Street.

Most of these firms have enjoyed exciting careers. Space limitations have made it necessary to omit many important happenings in the history of each firm. In some instances it has been difficult to establish the proper date for the beginning of the business. Some men started with a small mill and eventually joined a selling house. In other instances an individual or a selling house bought an early mill. The mill's history might go back many years.

Some firms began as individuals, or a partnership, while in other instances several members of a family began small individual businesses only to merge later. And again individuals or partners started businesses, later liquidated them, and then began again with new partners, thus breaking the chain in the history of the business. The "beginning dates" given on the following pages are those generally accredited to the organizations.

At least sixteen firms who have made Worth Street history are now over one hundred years old. The stories of these firms are told on the following pages, set down in alphabetical order.

JOSHUA L. BAILY & CO., INC. began business as a retail dry goods firm in Philadelphia under the name of Baily and Brother, but in 1845 changed to the wholesale dry goods field. Thereafter the senior member, Joshua L. Baily, was a member of firms whose individuals changed from time to time and whose organizations bore various designations, until the year 1876, when he established Joshua L. Baily and Company. This name has continued uninterruptedly until the present time, with the fourth generation of his descendants now engaged in the business.

Joshua L. Baily and Company's business expanded, and an office was established on Thomas Street, New York, in the Worth Street area, in 1880, with Charles H. Brooks as resident partner. Mr. Brooks' two sons, Charles and Elwood, subsequently were members of the firm.

Offices of the firm have been in the 40 Worth Street building since 1938, after having occupied space on Thomas Street for more than sixty years.

Other offices of Joshua L. Baily and Company were later established in the principal dry goods marketing centers throughout the United States, and for half a century the company has actively participated in export volume.

Joshua L. Baily lived to the ripe old age of ninety-one years. He spent his later years in philanthropic enterprises and was foremost in promoting temperance, having organized so-called Coffee Houses in Philadelphia where working men could obtain good food at reasonable prices and avoid the temptation of saloons and "free lunches."

BATES FABRICS, INC. was organized in 1937 by Herman Ruhm, George Aufderheide, William Lyall, Jr., and others from the old firm of Bliss Fabyan & Co., which began business in 1833.

The firm was originally owned by six stockholders: New England Industries Inc., Bates Manufacturing Co., and the four officers of the company, but in 1945 Bates Manufacturing Co., which was built in 1850, became the only stockholder, with Bates Fabrics, Inc. as a subsidiary.

Bates Fabrics, Inc. at first sold only bedspreads, tablecloths and sheets, but in 1945 it took over the personnel and the agency known as the Maine Mills and began distribution of the products of the Androscoggin, Edwards, Hill and York divisions, which were formerly individual companies whose principal stockholder was New England Industries.

Bates Fabrics, Inc. from its beginning has been located at 80 Worth Street, and occupies the building through to Thomas Street and also the 82 Worth Street Building. An interesting story developed around the number 80 after the firm also secured a telephone number 8080. The sequence of events so impressed one member of the firm with the magic of the number that he won a substantial amount on the "daily double" with it.

But their good luck did not run out with the loss of the number due to their expanding needs for more telephone equipment, for they are sometimes called "bedspread headquarters" and with colorful advertising and promotion, they are "spreading themselves around" in a big way now with a broad line of textile products.

One of the slogans of this important firm, "Loomed to be heirloomed," goes well with the attractive colonial design of their building.

BERKSHIRE FINE SPINNING ASSOCIATES, INC., which maintains its sales offices at 40 Worth Street, represents the consolidation in March 1929 of eight New England combed-goods manufacturers, all but one of whom had their origin before the turn of the century.

The oldest unit was the Coventry Company, established in 1805, with about 480 spindles, in Anthony, R.I., by members of the Anthony family. At that time there were probably

4500 spindles in America, most of them in Rhode Island.

In 1814 the Plunkett Mill was established in Adams, Mass., by the Plunkett family. In 1884 it became the Berkshire Cotton Manufacturing Company, under whose charter the present Berkshire operates. In those early days the goods woven in Adams were transported by oxcart to New Haven, Conn.

The Valley Falls Company had its beginning on the west bank of the Blackstone River at Albion, R.I., in 1818, and three of the original buildings are still in use as dwellings in the mill village, though moved from their original sites. This property was acquired in 1839 by Oliver Chace of Fall River, ancestor of the present president, Malcolm G. Chace, Jr.

The King Phillip Mills was incorporated in 1871. The Parker Mills, in Fall River, which included the Hargrave group, was established in 1895, while Fort Dummer Mills was built in 1908. In 1939 Berkshire acquired the yarn mill of the Farr Alpaca Company built in Holyoke, Mass., in 1920.

Historically, this is an interesting grouping of mills, one of which was among the first ten of the early pioneers dating back to the very beginning of the textile production in this country, while two other plants were built just after the War of 1812, when there was a shortage of textiles.

BORDEN MILLS, INC. was organized in 1924 as a wholly owned subsidiary of the American Printing Company of Fall River, Massachusetts. In 1925 a new mill building was completed in Kingsport, Tennessee, and approximately 100,000 spindles and 1,800 looms moved there from Fall River. The production of the plant was shipped to Fall River until 1934, when the American Printing Company ceased operation. Today it is a very modern plant and the production is sold in the open market.

The original Borden texile enterprise was the Anawan Manufactory, which was founded in Fall River, Mass., in 1825 by

Colonel Richard Borden, four years after he had started a prosperous iron business, the Fall River Iron Works. He also organized the Troy Cotton and Woolen Manufacturing Company, the American Print Works, the Fall River Line—the famous steamboat line running from Fall River to New York —and was active in banking and railroad affairs.

In 1865 M. C. D. Borden, youngest son of Richard Borden, started work with the jobbing house of Lathrop, Ludington & Co. in New York City. In 1868 he joined the commission house of Low, Harriman & Co., 65-67 Worth Street, selling agents for the American Print Works. In 1880 he transferred to Wright, Bliss and Fabyan, who became the selling agents for the American Print Works. In 1887, after the death of Colonel Richard Borden, he bought out other interests in the print works, absorbed the iron works and in 1889 built seven cotton mills. He was often referred to as the King of Calico because of his large operations. In 1897, a depression year, he boldly purchased a million dollars' worth of print cloth in a stagnant market. In 1910 he organized the commission house of M. C. D. Borden & Sons at 90 Worth Street, along with his sons, Bertram H. Borden and Howard S. Borden. In 1923 John C. Borden joined the firm and in 1929 Arthur B. Borden.

The business was continued until 1935, when the Iselin-Jefferson organization purchased the building and Borden Mills, Inc. became the Borden Division of Iselin-Jefferson Company, Inc.

CATLIN FARISH & CO., INC. began business in 1835 as Clark & Hunt at 60 Cedar Street as a dealer in dry goods. As a young man, Seth B. Hunt took a position with the firm of Arthur Tappan & Co. at the lower end of Pearl Street, one of the largest dry goods jobbing houses in the United States at that time, and later was joined by Israel W. Clark. This organization first introduced the cash and short-time credit system to the dry goods trade in New York.

In 1839 the firm became Hunt Brothers at 39 William Street, and in 1840 moved to 18 Exchange Place.

In 1860 the firm name was changed to Hunt, Tillinghast & Co. at 15 Park Place, and in 1872 became Seth B. Hunt & Co. at 70 Reade Street. By 1876 it was Hunt, Catlin & Valentine at 107 Franklin Street, and in 1880, Catlin & Co. at 216 Church Street, in 1901, at 345 Broadway. In 1886 the firm of Joy, Lincoln & Motley was absorbed, which firm had in 1882 taken over E. R. Mudge, Sawyer & Co. In 1897, the firm of O. H. Sampson & Co. was absorbed.

The firm of Farish-Stafford-Campbell Co. was organized in 1901 and during the same year changed its name to Farish-Stafford Co. at 61 Leonard Street. In 1908 it moved to 57 Worth Street and in 1912 to 110 Worth Street. In 1913 the name was changed to The Farish Company. In 1921 the firm moved to 83-85 Worth Street and in 1924 to 100 Worth Street. In 1927 it became selling agent for the Arnco Mills, the first new blanket mill built for making part-wool blankets on a modified wool system which eventually became the largest producer exclusively making that line. In 1928 it moved to its present building at 79-81 Worth Street. In 1929 it also became the selling agent for Arnall Mills, one of the early pioneer mills built in the 1860's as a small rope plant and later expanded to a large yarn mill, which, in turn, changed to cotton blankets to become the largest producer exclusively making that product.

In 1930, Catlin & Co., Inc. and The Farish Company merged into the present Catlin Farish Co., Inc. at 79 Worth Street, its present home.

CHICOPEE MILLS, INC. began business under this name in 1948 to handle the sales for the Chicopee group of mills. The company bought the building at 47 Worth Street in 1952 for its future home. W. J. Holman, Jr. is president.

The beginning of this business, however, dates back to

the Chicopee Manufacturing Corporation of Chicopee Falls, Mass., which began with the founding of the Boston and Springfield Manufacturing Company by a group of Boston capitalists, in, or shortly before, 1822. This company in that year began work on a dam, a canal and a cotton mill, with houses for the workers. The first mill was completed in 1825, the second begun in the same year, the third erected in 1826, the fourth in 1831. In 1828 the company changed its name to Chicopee Manufacturing Company. By 1832 it was employing 780 people and in 1835 had a capital of $750,000.

For many years prior to 1916 the production of the Chicopee Mills was sold in the Worth Street market by Minot Hooper & Co.

In 1916 Johnson & Johnson of New Brunswick, N.J., purchased the Chicopee Manufacturing Company and used most of the production in its operations until 1921, when Slocum & Company at 321 Broadway began to sell some of the production. This arrangement continued until 1927.

In that year, the Chicopee Sales Corporation began to sell the goods, having offices at 93 Worth Street, which were moved to 40 Worth Street in 1932 and to 47 Worth Street in 1945.

WM. E. HOOPER & SONS CO. was founded by William Hooper in association with a sailmaker named Hardester in about 1800. In 1845 Hardester's interests were purchased and the business was continued under the name of William Hooper.

In 1848 his son, William E. Hooper, continued the business and built the Woodberry Mill. By 1866 he owned the Mt. Washington, Park, Woodberry, Meadow and Clipper Mills, afterward purchasing the Druid Mill, operating them as the Woodberry Manufacturing Co., which he owned. His sons were taken into the business and the name was changed to Wm. E. Hooper & Sons Co.

Prior to 1875 their New York office was opened at 74 Broad Street. They later moved to 290 Broadway, in the

Worth Street area, and in 1916 to 320 Broadway, where the office is now located.

James E. Hooper became president in 1885 and built the present plant in 1904. His son, Robert P. Hooper, great-grandson of the founder, has been president since 1914.

ISELIN-JEFFERSON COMPANY, INC. began business in 1927 as a partnership between Oliver Iselin, representing the partnership of William Iselin & Co., and Floyd W. Jefferson, formerly an executive of the old Hunter Mfg. & Commission Co.

William Iselin & Co. dates its business back to 1808, when Isaac Iselin began business at 21 Broadway in the textile center on lower Manhattan, later moving to 84 Greenwich Street. From 1819 to 1823 the business was known as DeRham & Co., first at 77 and later at 86 Washington Street. In 1824 it became DeRham, Moore & Co. at 119 Pearl Street, and from 1828 to 1835 it was DeRham, Iselin and Moore at 44 Broad Street and 65 Murray Street. The great fire of 1835 destroyed their place of business along with others in the area. From 1836 to 1839 the firm name was Cottenet, H. Barbey and Co., 40 Broad Street, and Henry Barbey & Co. at 123 Pearl Street.

In 1840 Adrian Iselin, son of Isaac, began business as Moran & Iselin at 123 Pearl Street.

The firm moved to 47 Broad Street in 1848 and in 1854 became A. Iselin & Co. Successive removals to 46, then to 36 Barclay Street, and to Leonard Street, corner of Church Street, brought the dry goods business to the Worth Street area in 1864, although its banking business remained at 36 Wall Street until 1936.

On Leonard Street the firm name was first Giraud, Barbey & Co., but from 1864 to 1871 it was Henry Barbey & Co. By 1869 the firm was located at 339 Canal Street and at the adjoining corner on Greene Street. The name was again changed to Richard, Iselin & Co., 1871-1877; Iselin, Neeser & Co., 1877-1890, and to William Iselin & Co. in 1890, which name has continued to the present time. In 1913 the firm moved to 357 Fourth Avenue.

The firm has had a long and interesting career. The changes in name and in location showed the trend in these early days as small firms grew and expanded into larger ones.

The business began with importation of textiles from Austria, Belgium, England, France, Germany and Switzerland, but about 1885 it began to factor accounts, a needed service in an expanding textile field.

In 1878 it set up a Knit Goods Department and in 1911 a Cotton Piece Goods Department at 18 Thomas Street, which eventually became part of Iselin-Jefferson Company, Inc.

MINOT HOOPER CO., INC. began business under that style only recently, September 1951, with John Bowen as president, but the original business was started in 1840 as a partnership of George R. Minot and Nathaniel Hooper as Minot & Hooper at 32 India Wharf in Boston, Mass., to enter the shipping business. They were known as ships' cargo brokers, and as such found cargoes for ships in the East Indian and Orient trades. Textiles became a large part of the cargoes, and due to transactions with poorly financed mills it was not long before they were financially interested in some of them, which helped secure the needed cargoes for their ships.

The following advertisement in the Boston *Daily Advertiser* on January 1st, 1840, is interesting:

> The subscribers have formed a co-partnership under the firm name of Minot & Hooper for the transaction of Commission business at No. 32 India Wharf. Usual advances made on consignments.
>
> Boston, Jan'y 1st, 1840 *George R. Minot*
> *Nath'l Hooper*

In 1866, the firm name was changed to Minot Hooper & Company, and in 1867 it opened an office in New York at 53 Leonard Street. In 1896 it moved to 40 Thomas Street, and in 1909 to 11 Thomas Street and 82 Worth Street. In 1931 the offices were moved to 40 Worth Street.

George Nichols will be remembered by many as the Commodore of the New York Yacht Club in 1924, and owner of the famous boat *Goose* with which he captured the Scandinavian Gold Cup in 1938 and many other trophies. John W. T. Nichols was very active in market circles for several years.

Minot Hooper & Co. was the first American house to export cotton piece goods to the Levant, and the brand name of the Dwight Mfg. Co., Cabot "A" Sheeting, became so well known that the natives in those countries used the word "Cabot" to describe all unbleached sheeting fabrics.

PACIFIC MILLS began business in 1850 in Boston with James Little, who was head of the firm of Little-Alden & Company, as one of the original incorporators. This latter firm had a branch office later on in the Worth Street market and was the selling agent for the Pacific Mills. Later the firm name was changed to James L. Little & Company, and continued to sell the product until 1883, when Lawrence & Company of 24 Thomas Street became the agents.

In 1926 Pacific set up its own sales agency at 24 Thomas Street and later at 40 Worth Street, but in 1951 moved to 1407 Broadway, where they are at present located.

As far back as 1885, Pacific was producing 100,000,000 yards of goods a year, more than any other mill at the time. By 1925 it was producing 315,000,000 yards. For forty-three years the production was sold by Lawrence & Company on the site of the present Merchants Club.

An interesting story is told of the change from Little & Company to Lawrence & Company. Differences over one thing and another developed between Mr. Little, a partner in the mill and also its selling agent, and Mr. Lawrence, a partner in the mill and part of the mill management. In time, even the directors became divided.

A difference arose over whether to make a stripe fabric with four ends of color or six ends. The dispute reached the top when Little said six ends and Lawrence four. Finally the looms shut down and the dispute went before a directors' meeting. In the showdown, some directors said four and some six, while others accused them all of "splitting threads."

Then Little said he would resign unless he could make it with six threads, and after much debate a vote of directors accepted his resignation. Later arrangements were made with Lawrence & Company to handle the sales, and a big account changed sales agencies over a matter of two threads in a stripe of only one of their fabrics.

It is said that when this very large account was offered to Lawrence & Company, Amos Lawrence, instead of celebrating, resorted to prayer, for in his diary he wrote: "January 6, 1883. The Pacific Mills . . . . have offered to my firm the direction of their vast business, the largest in the United States. May God direct us to a right decision; and if we undertake it, may He give us success and wisdom to use the results in His service, and not in selfish gratification; so that we, and our children after us, may not be damaged by it. Amen."

Thus was expressed the spirit of the old Worth Street.

PARKER, WILDER & CO., INC. relates the beginning of its business in Boston in an interesting way.

It is an April afternoon in the year 1820. A light breeze ripples in through the forest of masts in Boston Harbor. It searches the decks of packets and Indiamen. It discovers pleasant odors of fruits and coffee and orient spices. It captures the tang of fragrant teas, of pungent sandalwood and teak. Then it bears the mingled scents shoreward, mixed with the smell of tarred rope and the briny rumor of the sea.

At the foot of Broad Street, hard by the harbor's Long Wharf, a freshly painted sign is drying in the spring air. Its legend announces, from over the door of a business house, that a new enterprise has been born. The project will grow and flourish greatly in the years ahead. Yet the sign says, simply enough:

ISAAC PARKER & CO.

NO. 6 BROAD ST.

Extensive Assortment
of American Goods
for Sale

Isaac Parker's father, Abel Parker, had been a Minute Man from Pepperell who, when the alarm of Lexington sounded, left his plow and hurried to battle and later was wounded at Bunker Hill. He became a man of great distinction.

Isaac was born in New Hampshire and began work in a local store at the age of fourteen. In 1809 he set up the firm of Parker & Hugh. He helped to found the Peterborough Factory, and in 1817 went to Boston to form the firm of Bullard & Parker at 31 Central Street. Three years later, at the age of thirty-two, he founded the business of Parker, Wilder & Company, offering a badly needed service, that of commission merchant, to the developing New England mill industry. At the time the markets were flooded with foreign-made goods, and the small scattered mills were facing extinction and badly needed financing as well as help and advice.

The business prospered and in 1831 moved to larger quarters at 74 Water Street. In 1837 it became Parker, Blanchard and Wilder Company, and in 1842, Parker, Wilder, and Parker when the eldest son of the founder entered the firm. In 1850 the name was again changed to Parker, Wilder & Company, and in 1856 moved to 67 Federal Street. In 1858 Isaac Parker was killed in a carriage accident, something which the present generation accustomed to speed would hardly believe possible.

In 1861 the firm opened a branch office in Worth Street and its Boston office moved to 4 Winthrop Square.

In 1931 the firm moved its headquarters to 215 Fourth Avenue, New York, but maintains an office at 40 Worth Street.

On April 1, 1946, the firm was incorporated, and Mr. George A. Adam became its first president, having been a partner for thirty-nine years.

PEPPERELL MANUFACTURING COMPANY opened selling offices under its own name in 1928 at 40 Worth Street. The mill product, however, was first offered in New York in 1851, when its Boston selling agent, Francis Skinner & Co., began selling some of its production through its branch office at 2 College Place, now West Broadway at Barclay Street.

The Pepperell Mill had been built in 1850 in Biddeford, Maine, being named for Sir William Pepperell who earlier had owned a small mill there and considerable land on the Saco River. The mill promptly appointed Francis Skinner & Co. of Boston as its selling agents, which arrangements continued until 1870, at which date the agency was selling for such mills as Pepperell, James, Bates, Porter, Franklin, Kennebec, Portland, Uncasville, Portsmouth, Central Mills, Burlington, Otter River, North Vassalboro, Wamsetta (not Wamsutta), Laconia, Androscoggin and Continental. In that year Francis Skinner & Co. ran into financial difficulties and Pepperell appointed J. S. & E. Wright & Co., another Boston firm, as its selling agents.

By 1882 this latter firm had become Bliss Fabyan & Co., with Cornelius N. Bliss and George F. Fabyan as senior partners. The New York office was on Franklin Street, and later Thomas Street. This venerable firm finally closed up in 1940, but in the meantime Pepperell had set up its offices in 1928, as mentioned above.

J. P. STEVENS & CO., INC. began business in 1946, but the original business was started in 1813 when the founder,

Nathaniel Stevens, built a small woolen mill in Andover, Mass. He was evidently encouraged by the action of this small town which in the year 1787, the year that the American Constitution was written, passed the following resolution:

> We hereby resolve to refrain from as far as in our power, to prevent the excessive use and consumption of articles of foreign manufacture, and we will exert our best endeavors for the promotion of industry and our own manufactures. And, in particular, that we will exert ourselves to increase our wool and flax as far as practicable, that we will, as far as may be, avoid killing our sheep, or killing them for slaughter after shearing them, till the wool be serviceable for clothing. And that we will exert ourselves to promote and encourage the manufactures of wool and flax and other raw materials into such articles as shall be useful in the community.

The little company used not more than fifty pounds of wool per day and made woolen flannels on hand looms. After the War of 1812, all businesses experienced a difficult time. The new mill started with very little money and after ten years its account book, which has been preserved, shows that the total assets of the business were valued at $12,402. By 1829 the assets had grown to $35,179, and by 1833 to $60,354.

In 1830 Nathaniel Stevens bought a bell for the mill from a church in Castine, Maine. It had been cast by the Revere Copper Company in 1804, when Paul Revere was head of the company. The bell is still in use on the present mill.

In 1850 the business name was changed to Nathaniel Stevens & Son, and in 1855 the Pentucket Mill was acquired in Haverhill, Mass., the first step in expansion. In 1870 another woolen mill was purchased, at Franklin Falls, N.H.

In 1876 the company name was changed to M. T. Stevens, and in 1879 it bought the Marland Mills built in 1807, which, in effect, gave the organization a "beginning date" of 1807. In 1885 the name was changed to M. T. Stevens & Sons when

Nathaniel and Samuel, sons of Moses T. Stevens, were taken
into the business.

Up to this time the product of these mills had been sold
through several selling agents, but in 1899 a partnership was
formed with $25,000 capital to establish a selling house, which
was set up at 23-25 Thomas Street in the Worth Street district.
Later it moved to 44 Leonard Street.

In 1921 and 1923 Robert T. and John P. Stevens, Jr., sons
of John P. Stevens, joined J. P. Stevens & Co. In 1945 Robert
T. Stevens became chairman and John P. Stevens, Jr., president of the company. It is today one of the largest textile organizations in the country, with offices since 1952 in the Stevens
Building at 1410 Broadway. Robert Stevens became Secretary
of the Army in 1953.

WELLINGTON SEARS COMPANY originated in Boston
in 1845, when Nehemiah Boynton founded the firm of Boynton
and Miller, ship chandlers. The company, known as N. Boynton after 1852, sold ships' supplies, the principal item being
canvas for sails. The heavier canvas was marked with the picture of a duck, and later such fabrics became known as "ducks."

In 1856, near the end of the clipper ship era, N. Boynton
& Company became selling agents for the Russell Mills, duck
manufacturers of Plymouth, Massachusetts, and in 1887 for the
West Point Manufacturing Company, West Point, Georgia.

No longer ship chandlers, N. Boynton & Company had been
long established as textile merchants when a New York office,
now sales headquarters, was opened at Worth and Church
Streets in 1900. In 1901 the name was changed to Wellington,
Sears & Company, the partners being William H. Wellington,
Horace S. Sears and Edward P. Boynton. Over the years the
cotton ducks were supplemented by a broad range of other
industrial fabrics. A line of apparel fabrics, originally developed for the work clothing industry, later expanded into
the sportswear field and, most recently, into women's sport

fashions—highlighted, appropriately enough, by the popular sailcloth, "Topsail."

The well-known line of Martex towels was taken over in 1928, to which later was added the Fairfax line.

Incorporated in 1931 as Wellington Sears Company, Inc., the company was acquired by the West Point Manufacturing Company in 1945.

GEORGE WOOD, SONS & CO. was originally organized in 1872 as R. D. Wood & Sons, with its New York office at 106 Franklin Street, where it is still located after 80 years. The current name was adopted in 1912.

David C. Wood, the founder, started an iron foundry at Millville, N.J., about 1804 to process the Jersey bog iron ore, a low-grade ore found in the Jersey swamps. Jersey pine trees were used as charcoal for fuel. In 1840 the business was taken over by his younger half-brother, Richard D. Wood. In 1842 he built the present Millville Cotton Mill with the idea at the time of giving employment to the wives and children of his iron workers. A bleachery was built in 1863, and in 1869 another cotton mill at May's Landing, about fifteen miles away. The present Millville Mfg. Company has been operated by the Wood family for 148 years.

WOODWARD, BALDWIN & CO., INC. first began business on May 8, 1828, as the partnership of Jones & Woodward, conducting a wholesale dry goods and commission business in Baltimore, Md.

In 1844 the firm name was changed to William Woodward & Company, and in 1865 to Woodward, Baldwin & Co. For a short time in 1870 the Baltimore business operated as Woodward, Baldwin & Norris, while the New York office operated under the name of Woodward, Baldwin & Co. It remained as a partnership until 1947, when the business was incorporated.

Woodward, Baldwin & Co. opened an office in the Worth Street area in 1863 on Duane Street, but shortly thereafter moved to its present location at 43 to 45 Worth Street, where it has remained for over 80 years.

The company's license issued in 1828 for doing business in Baltimore is not only an historic document but an interesting one to read.

STORE LICENSE
(*Not Transferable*)

BALTIMORE CITY COURT, FEBRUARY TERM, 1828

LICENSE is hereby granted to Jones & Woodward to Deal in any "kind of Goods, Wares or Merchandise, foreign or domestic," at their Store, No. 229½ Market Street, within the City of Baltimore. This License to continue "UNTIL THE FIRST DAY OF MAY NEXT," unless sooner Suppressed for a violation of the Laws of this State in such case provided.

This License authorizes the person or persons obtaining it to Retail "Spirituous or Fermented Liquor," but not in less quantities than TEN GALLONS AT ONE TIME, under a Law passed at December Session, 1827, entitled "An Act to regulate the issuing of Licenses to Traders, Keepers of Ordinaries and others."

Test, *Wm. M. Medcalf*

$12.00   8th May 1828

From this license it will be seen that the firm was authorized to sell goods of any kind, foreign and domestic, as well as "spirituous or fermented liquor" provided it sold not less than 10 gallons at one time.

CHAPTER XXVI

Men, Merchants and Mills

While the age of a firm or its mills has an historic significance, this alone does not determine the part it has played in the development of Worth Street or its contribution to a better textile world. The histories of the firms which follow are interesting and important in many ways. Some have been in business for seventy-five years, some for fifty and some for twenty-five. Some are made up of individuals who were formerly with one of the older firms and are experienced merchants in the Street. Other firms organized more recently have mills which have long and honorable records of their own, having been merchandised formerly through other Worth Street houses. As in the preceding chapter, the histories of these organizations will be taken up in alphabetical order.

AMERICAN BLEACHED GOODS COMPANY, INC. began business in 1942, but the original business was started in 1909 as American Bleached Goods Company at 39 Leonard Street, with Edmund S. Twining as president. William F. Adam became president in 1919, and in 1928 the company moved to 40 Worth Street.

In 1929 the affiliated companies Lorraine Manufacturing Company and Kelsey Wilton Textile Corp. joined with American Bleached Goods Company in the formation of Federated Textiles, Inc. as selling agents for their various products.

In 1941 James L. Geoffroy was elected president, and in the following year American began the distribution of its own products under the name of American Bleached Goods Company, Inc. In 1948 N. Ross MacCallum was elected president.

This firm records an interesting historical event in that the fabric used to cover the wings of the first airplane flown by the Wright Brothers was their "Pride of the West Muslin."

WILLIAM L. BARRELL COMPANY was incorporated in 1904 by William L. Barrell, who had previously operated the Lawrence Duck Company, Lawrence, Mass., and who had acquired the Abingdon Mill of Huntsville, Ala., predecessor to the present Lincoln Mills of Alabama. The announced purpose of the enterprise was to merchandise cotton fabrics, particularly cotton ducks and canvas, in both gray and finished state, and to act as commission selling agents.

Since its beginning the company has always been in the Worth Street district, commencing at 89 Worth Street, where Fred S. Bennett was in charge of operations. While the home office has been maintained in Boston, the merchandising center is at present at 40 Worth Street.

The officers of the company are Charles D. McDuffie, president, and Sallo M. Kahn, executive vice president.

It is interesting to note that twenty per cent of the present staff of the company have been associated with it for periods of time ranging from twenty-five to forty-eight years. There has always been a member of the Barrell family connected with the company, and at present three grandsons of the founder are actively associated with it.

JOHN BOYLE & COMPANY, INC. was founded in 1860 by John Boyle, who came to this country from England. The business first started on Furman Street in Brooklyn, but later moved to Manhattan, where it occupied the premises at 199 to 207 Fulton Street until 1905. In that year it moved to 112 to 114 Duane Street, where it is still domiciled.

John Boyle is believed to have originated the idea of using striped fabrics for awnings in the United States, and his patterns were sold all over the country as well as abroad.

The firm also has made mailbags, tents, tarpaulins and army equipment from various types of textiles since as far back as the Civil War. At one time the firm made the tents for the Barnum and Bailey Circus.

CALLAWAY MILLS, INC., one of the members of the Association of Cotton Textile Merchants, 40 Worth Street, is the selling house for Callaway Mills Company, LaGrange, Georgia. This latter company is the successor to Callaway Mills, which were originally started in 1900 by the late Fuller E. Callaway.

Prior to 1922, when Callaway Mills, Inc. was organized, the production of these mills was sold by J. H. Lane & Co. at 110 Worth Street.

In 1947 the Callaway family, who were in control of the Company, decided to liquidate the business.

The mills had been previously sold to a foundation, and since 1947 the entire stock of Callaway Mills Company, the operating Company, has been owned by Callaway Community Foundation. This, briefly, means that the mills, operating Company, and sales organization are now owned by a foundation. The operating Company operates as a regular corporation paying regular corporation taxes, but the stock of same is owned by the Foundation.

CANNON MILLS, INC. was formed in September 1920, as a wholly owned subsidiary of the Cannon Manufacturing Co. of Kannapolis, N. C. The firm was originally located at 55 Worth Street, but moved to 70 Worth Street, its present quarters, in 1924.

Cannon Mills, Inc., of which Stanley Phillips is president,

serves as selling agents both for Cannon Mills Company and for fifteen independent mills.

The Cannon Manufacturing Company was started in 1887 by James William Cannon at Concord, N. C. Its chief product was coarse cotton yarn. Later followed the development of the branded "Cannon Cloth" used in the South for women's and children's clothing. In 1889 cotton crash towels were added to the line.

Success brought about expansion. Mr. Cannon built a mill at Concord in 1900, where the first Cannon cotton terry towel was produced. In 1906 the first of the mills at Kannapolis, N. C., was erected.

During this time all products of the Cannon Manufacturing Company were sold through Worth Street commission houses. In 1903 Mr. Cannon opened his own selling agency in New York City, at 53 Leonard Street, with Mr. John C. Leslie as manager. In 1905 this selling office moved to 55 Worth Street, and later to 70 Worth Street. In 1928 Cannon Mills Company was formed, resulting from the merger of Cannon Manufacturing Company and several cotton mills in which Mr. Cannon was interested and for which Cannon Mills, Inc. had been selling agents.

Following the death of James William Cannon in 1921, his son, Charles A. Cannon, became president of all Cannon enterprises. Some outstanding landmarks in Cannon's growth include the first trade-paper advertising in 1921; the first towels with Cannon labels sewed on in 1923, and the first Cannon consumer advertising in 1924. Merchandise decoration began cautiously with a few towel styles made with colored borders. From then on, Cannon gradually introduced color into its complete line. Subsequent consumer advertising began to feature towels in matched sets.

Today, Cannon Mills is the world's largest manufacturer of household textiles, with a complete line of towels, sheets, bedspreads, draperies and decorating fabrics.

CONE MILLS, INC., until June 2, 1952, Cone Export and Commission Co., Inc., was organized in 1891 by Moses H. and Ceasar Cone to market the products of about fifty Southern cotton mills at a time when textile production and distribution in the South was disorganized.

Herman Cone, the father of the founders, landed in Richmond in 1845 and by 1856 was operating a general store in Jonesboro, Tenn., where he was selling dry goods and getting his first experience with textiles.

By 1869 he was established in the wholesale grocery business in Baltimore under the firm name of Cone & Adler, which by 1870 became H. Cone and Sons. Five of his sons were in the business and were the salesmen who traveled extensively from Maryland to Alabama.

In those days wholesale grocers also sold cotton plaids, in great demand in the South, where every crossroad store bought them in bale lots; so again the Cones were selling cotton goods.

In 1887 they gave up the wholesale grocery business to pioneer in textiles.

They became interested in a mill in Asheville, N. C., which eventually became the Asheville Cotton Mills in 1892, the first Cone mill and still part of their chain. According to the company's record there were fifty-odd mills in the South in 1890, and 95 per cent of their production was cotton plaids.

The firm opened an office in the Worth Street area in 1891, located later at 89 Worth Street and subsequently at 74 to 76 Worth Street. In 1928 it erected a very modern office building at 59 Worth Street, which it still occupies. Herman Cone is chairman and Saul F. Dribben is president of this organization, which dates its textile experience back to 1856.

The story is told that the Cone brothers finally became imbued with the idea that the farmer and the workingman did not have a suitable fabric for a strictly working garment, and they wanted to develop one. The idea grew and expanded year after year as better fabrics were made, until finally they produced a high-grade blue denim which today meets the requirements for a work and utility garment.

Fate carried the blue denim from the farm and factory to Main Street, where the "bobby soxers" delighted in rolling their pants to the knees, and a fastidious public took the "blue jeans" on to Fifth Avenue and Hollywood. In this way a pioneering vision came true beyond the fondest dreams.

The Cone mills are now the largest producers of denim and cotton flannels in the world, and make a large variety of cotton materials for work, play and household uses, as well as fabrics of man-made fibers.

DAN RIVER MILLS, INC. of Danville, Va., was set up under this name in 1946, but the name of the original mill was the Riverside Cotton Mills, organized in 1882, and later changed to Riverside & Dan River Cotton Mills, Inc., after the merger in 1909 of the Riverside Cotton Mills and the Dan River Power & Manufacturing Company.

In 1891 the mill opened its selling office in the Worth Street District at 34 Thomas Street, but in 1908 moved to 56 Worth Street. In 1928 it moved to 46 Worth Street, and in 1931 to 40 Worth Street. In 1950 it moved to 1407 Broadway.

In the beginning, the Riverside Cotton Mills had six stockholders, a capital of $75,000, and 2,240 spindles and 100 looms. It is interesting to note that these stockholders were Dr. H. W. Cole, a druggist; B. F. Jefferson, a coal, wood and lumber dealer; Thomas B. Fitzgerald, a contractor and brick maker; John H. Schoolfield, a merchant and tobacco manufacturer; James E. Schoolfield, a hardware merchant; and Robert A. Schoolfield, who became the manager. They organized the mill without any knowledge of the textile business.

Just what induced them to start the venture is unknown, but it was a success and today has 6,500 stockholders.

DEERING, MILLIKEN & CO. was founded in 1865 in New York before the close of the Civil War by Seth M. Milliken and William Deering, who had earlier been associated in business in Portland, Maine. Mr. Milliken began his career as a merchant at the family home in Minot, Maine, where, after teaching at Hebron Academy, he operated a general store. He was less than thirty years of age when he came to New York.

The first location in New York was near 79 Worth Street, where, Mr. Milliken said in after years, he was his own office boy and a dry goods box was his desk. That statement tells the story of Worth Street, for like others he came to the district with a fixed purpose to enter the textile business and a determination to make a success of it. Textiles, production and distribution were intriguing to the minds of young men with ambition, for there was pioneering work to be done in an era when the country was turning from imported goods to domestic goods and the industry from hand machines to power machines. "His own office boy" and a "dry goods box for a desk" expressed a serious determination to build a business soundly.

Before 1870 Mr. Deering left his friend and established the Deering Harvester Company in Chicago, later to become a part of The International Harvester Company.

As the business in New York grew rapidly under the guidance of this long-visioned pioneer, it occupied larger quarters, first at 53 and later at 79 Leonard Street.

An early story about Mr. Milliken's career has him riding every day from his home uptown to his Worth Street office in his own carriage, wearing his high top hat and cutaway coat, a quaint custom of the day but the proper dress for a successful merchant.

In later years, the company changed from a partnership to a corporation and expanded rapidly. It is one of the largest textile organizations in the country today. Its present quarters in the Worth Street district, 240 Church Street, is the last word in modern building, constructed along the lines of a bank or institution, but appropriate for its purpose and in keeping with the status of this pioneer organization, which, as it will readily admit, is still pioneering.

FIELDCREST MILLS was the name adopted in 1947 for the manufacturing division of Marshall Field & Co. to clearly identify the mills with the nationally advertised Fieldcrest brand name. The original mill division began business, however, in 1902, when Marshall Field & Co. of Chicago decided to enter the textile manufacturing field to supply goods to its wholesale concern, which was then expanding its business.

The company at first made a contract with the American Warehousing Corporation, which operated seven mills at Spray and Draper, N. C., to take the entire production. A few years later, due to general conditions, these mills could not continue operation, and Marshall Field & Co. acquired them. A subsidiary mill company was set up, the Carolina Cotton and Woolen Mill Corporation, during the life of the wholesale division. The plants were not only modernized and expanded but additional plants were built to round out the organization.

When Marshall Field & Co. liquidated the wholesale division, the mill organization set up sales offices in the mid-1930's for the nationwide distribution of its products.

GREENWOOD MILLS, INC. began business in 1946 when Jas. C. Self, J. B. Harris, Marvin Cross and others set up the new organization to handle sales for the Self Mills, which in earlier days had been handled by the old Hunter Manufacturing and Commission Company and to which other units have been added more recently.

This organization in 1952 bought and virtually rebuilt the two six-story buildings at 62/64 Worth Street and 31/33

Thomas Street, giving it one of the most modern homes in the Worth Street district. The two modernized buildings now have green brick-and-glass fronts and are air-conditioned throughout. The inside walls on the lower floor are finished with a textile fabric.

James C. Self began his career as a clerk in a small country store at $8.00 per week, and later became cashier of the Bank of Greenwood. It is said that J. B. Duke, of American Tobacco Co. fame, once said to him as cashier of the bank, "You'll never get anywhere lending $50 on a blind mule." He took that advice, became president of the bank and of the Greenwood Cotton Mills, and went on to build one of the largest textile organizations of the South.

The original mill was organized in 1890 as a local project when individuals bought most of the stock on a weekly installment basis paying fifty cents to one dollar per week on each $100 subscription. The mill had 2500 spindles and produced sheeting.

Another mill in the group, the Ninety Six Cotton Mill, was built in 1902 at Ninety Six, S. C. This village with its peculiar name was one of the early trading posts between the whites who had settled in lower South Carolina and the Indians to the west. An old legend says that a white trader's son and an Indian maiden had fallen in love, and when the maiden heard plans of her tribe to massacre those at the trading post, she rode a horse ninety-six miles from her mountain village to warn her lover. The community was saved and adopted the unusual name to commemorate the occasion.

It is interesting that a church in one of the Greenwood Mill villages has the famous carillon bells and the tower which the Dutch government sent to the New York World's Fair in 1939. Mr. Self bought them at the Fair for the village church.

Today the Greenwood organization, with its very modern plants, is doing a diversified business in combed and carded cotton fabrics, and rayons and synthetics.

HESSLEIN & CO., INC. began business at 75 Worth Street in 1923 as a selling agency for domestic mills, with Edgar J. Hesslein as chairman and Frank L. Walton, president. With some change in personnel, it has continued to the present time as a wholly owned subsidiary of Neuss Hesslein & Co., Inc. of the same address, with George W. Walker as the present president.

The beginning of this business dates back to 1865, when Samuel A. Hesslein founded a single proprietorship under his name. In the same year Edward Neuss acquired an interest, and the enterprise became known as Neuss and Hesslein.

In the early years the firm was engaged largely in importing textiles from Europe, but in 1874 an Export Department specializing in cotton textiles was added.

In 1893 the founder retired and his son, Edgar J. Hesslein, came into the firm, together with the late Eugene O. Beyer. Mr. Neuss retired soon after and was succeeded by John Staudt.

The company was incorporated in 1919, but down to the present date the Hesslein, Beyer and Staudt families continue as principal stockholders, although in 1928 they made gifts of a portion of their stock holdings for the benefit of the employees.

With the passing of Mr. Hesslein, John K. Whitaker, who had commenced his employment with the company in 1912 at the age of fifteen, was elected president, in which position he continued until his death in 1948, when Hugo H. Riedl, also the managing director of the company's Manchester (England) subsidiary, became the company's third president. In 1953 George W. Walker became president.

The company is the largest exporter of cotton piece goods from the United States, and is actively engaged in the export of British-made goods from England, where it owns several mills and a bleachery.

A. D. JUILLIARD & CO., INC. first began business in 1874 when Augustus D. Juilliard formed a partnership of A. D. Juilliard & Co. with D. E. Mackenzie, with whom he had been associated in Hoyt, Spragues & Co., which firm had gone out of business. At that time the firm was located at 65 Worth Street, later moving to 70 Worth Street and 19-23 Thomas Street.

For fifty years the firm remained in Worth Street, where it was one of the large and historic firms distributing the product of a number of important mills. In 1924, due partly to a change in the type of its products, the firm moved to new headquarters at 40 West 40th Street.

A. D. Juilliard was well known as a textile man, but also for his great interest in music. He set up the Juilliard Music Foundation.

THE KENDALL MILLS moved to 40 Worth Street when the present building was erected on that site in 1928. The firm is a division of The Kendall Company of Boston, which began business in 1903 at Walpole, Mass., when Henry P. Kendall took over a small mill, the Lewis Batting Company, which among a few other things was making absorbent cotton. It was an antiquated plant, for the cotton was dried on chicken wire over boxed-in steam coils through which air was blown. A small modernization program soon followed. The name was changed to the Lewis Manufacturing Company, and gauze was added to the line. In 1928 the firm name was changed to The Kendall Company. Several plants were purchased and others expanded, until the present organization consists of thirteen plants in six states and plants in Canada, Cuba and Mexico.

One of its subsidiaries, Pelzer Mills, has a long record in the Worth Street market. It was incorporated in South Carolina in 1880, and the product distributed until 1923 by Woodward Baldwin & Company and until 1930 by Lawrence & Company.

In 1896 the Pelzer Mills constructed a hydroelectric plant on the Saluda River about four miles from the mills. It was erected under the direct supervision of the late Dr. Charles P. Steinmetz of General Electric Company. Pelzer says it was the first plant in the country to be driven by electricity generated several miles away.

J. H. LANE & COMPANY, INC. was organized in 1888 by J. H. Lane, James W. Lane and F. Coit Johnson.

For twenty-four years the business was located at 110 Worth Street, where it sold the product of a number of important mills and added greatly to the history of Worth Street.

In 1912 the firm moved to 334 Fourth Avenue, and in 1922 to its present offices at 250 West 57th Street. F. Huntington Babcock is president at the present time.

LESLIE & CO. was started in 1945 at 39 Thomas Street by Frank H. Leslie and Henry M. Leslie, Jr., and later moved to 40 Worth Street.

The original firm began in 1906 at 61 Leonard Street under the name of Baldwin & Leslie. The partners were Carroll Baldwin and Henry M. Leslie, with William E. Wall as special partner.

This firm continued until the death of Carroll Baldwin in 1917, when the firm of Leslie, Evans & Co. was formed with William E. Evans as partner, and continued until 1945.

The firm has consistently been a gray-goods organization throughout its career.

M. LOWENSTEIN & SONS, INC. originally began business in 1889 as M. Lowenstein & Sons, when its balance sheet showed a net worth of $2,500, a meager beginning for a firm now listed on the New York Stock Exchange.

The business started as jobbers and importers of various lines at 7 Lispenard Street and later at 13 Lispenard Street. Leon Lowenstein joined the firm, which he now heads, in 1899 at the latter location. It was around that time that the firm decided one day to put their own name on bleached goods instead of selling under a mill brand name, which started them in the converting business. The business grew and expanded to include 15 Lispenard Street and eventually moved to Houston Street, corner of Mercer Street.

In 1904, a partnership was formed of M. Lowenstein and his two sons, and the firm moved to 40 West 23rd Street. After several years the firm moved back to the Worth Street area at 43 Leonard Street, where it now owns its own home.

In 1918 the business was incorporated, and in 1929 began its first move toward integration with the building of the Rock Hill Printing and Finishing Company. It began to buy gray-goods mills in 1944 to further the integration process, and today is a completely integrated organization.

Recently the firm bought a site at Broadway and Fortieth Street, where it will later make its headquarters.

McCAMPBELL & COMPANY was incorporated and started business in the Worth Street area in January 1923 at 320 Broadway, as a department of Harding Tilton & Company, which undertook the factoring of the business. The firm was formed by a group of five individuals, Leavelle McCampbell, Bryant McCampbell, Raymond H. Storm, John G. Brodie and John C. Hughes, to merchandise and distribute the product of several mills previously sold through Converse & Company.

In late December 1927 McCampbell & Company began

operation as an independent selling agent handling its own accounts. In 1938 it moved its offices from 320 Broadway to 40 Worth Street, where it is still located.

Leavelle McCampbell (who died in February 1946) was one of those who contributed greatly to the setting up of the Worth Street Rules, and was also quite active in the Merchants Club.

The Graniteville Company which is represented by this firm is one of the oldest mills in America, having been started in 1845.

REEVES BROTHERS, INC. began business in 1920 as a partnership, having been organized by M. R. Reeves and John M. Reeves.

The beginning of this business really dates back, however, to 1914, when M. R. Reeves, an executive of the old Hunter Manufacturing and Commission Co., left that organization to set up his own department with the firm of Harding Tilton Company at 66 Leonard Street. In 1919 M. R. Reeves and David Jennings formed a partnership known as Reeves-Jennings and Company at 55 Leonard Street. At the end of 1920 this partnership was dissolved and the partnership of Reeves Brothers formed, made up of M. R. Reeves and John M. Reeves, who withdrew from the Hunter Manufacturing and Commission Co. In 1922 the business was incorporated and in 1928 moved to 40 Worth Street.

In 1936 the firm moved to 54 Worth Street, and later it bought the building at this address. At various intervals it took over the firms of Kerr and Callaghan, Eagle Neckband Company, W. Harris Thurston Co., and acquired several mills and finishing plants. The Eagle & Phenix Mills, one of its units, dates back to 1850, and is one of the historic cotton mills in the hundred-year class.

Reeves Brothers Company, Inc. developed the famous Byrd cloth for Admiral Richard Byrd and his polar expeditions, and the cloth is now being sold for general outerwear use. Admiral Byrd is a member of the Board of Directors.

SIMTEX MILLS, a division of the Simmons Co., was set up in 1946 at 40 Worth Street with Richard C. Pohlers as its head.

This organization began in the early 1890's when James L. Wilson and James W. Cooke organized James L. Wilson and Company, with its main office at 239 Chestnut Street in Philadelphia and a New York office at 48 Leonard Street.

In 1928 the firm name became Rosemary Sales Corporation, with C. A. Pohlers as president, and in 1935 was Rosemary, Inc.

In 1943, it became Rosemary Sales, Division of the Simmons Company.

SOUTHEASTERN COTTONS, INC. began business in 1933 with Howard E. Coffin as chairman and Frederick H. Payne as president at 58-60 Worth Street, its present location.

The company was set up to take over a portion of the business of the old Hunter Mfg. & Commission Co., which went out of business at that time.

The Hunter Co. firm had been incorporated in 1906, and first had its offices at 69 Leonard Street, but in 1909 moved to 58-60 Worth Street.

In 1946 Avondale Mills of Sylacauga, Ala., and Cowikee Mills of Eufaula, Ala., purchased the entire stock of Southeastern Cottons, Inc. Donald Comer, Sr., became chairman and Donald Comer, Jr., president.

In 1949 the company purchased the land and building at 58-60 Worth Street and at 35-37 Thomas Street.

The original Avondale Mill was built in Birmingham, Ala., in 1897 by B. B. Comer, a former Governor of Alabama and one of its outstanding citizens.

Donald Comer, Sr., the present chairman of the executive committee of the mill, has carried on the old tradition and is today one of the outstanding leaders not only of the textile field but in many other fields of activity.

Hugh Comer, the chairman of the board of the mill, is one of the most sought-after speakers in the country today and is spreading textile cheer wherever he goes. J. Craig Smith, who is president, is very active in several mill associations.

TURNER HALSEY COMPANY, INC. began business in 1908 as an outgrowth of the old J. Spencer Turner Company when L. Hamilton Turner, a nephew of J. Spencer Turner, and C. D. W. Halsey organized the firm at 9 Thomas Street to take over the converting department of the J. Spencer Turner Co. George M. Miller was with the department at the time and joined the new firm. Turner became its first president and Halsey the secretary and treasurer.

In 1911 C. D. W. Halsey became president, and in 1914 Spencer Turner and Harold M. Turner, grandsons of J. Spencer Turner, joined the company, the former as vice-president. George M. Miller became manager of the converted goods division.

J. Spencer Turner was one of the founders of the Mt. Vernon-Woodberry Mills of Baltimore, and through Turner Halsey Company the third generation of the family continued its active interest in the mill and the production and sale of cotton duck and heavy cotton fabrics.

The Baltimore units of the mills began business in 1810, and a large unit at Tallassee, Ala., dates back to the first half of the last century, so that these mills were early pioneers in the textile industry.

In 1810, there were only a few mills in existence in this country. Howard Baetjer, prominent in the textile industry for many years, was president of this group of mills from 1914 to 1946, when he was succeeded by Thomas M. Bancroft, who had been treasurer of Turner Halsey Co. and in charge of their synthetic fabric division.

C. D. W. Halsey is honorary chairman of Turner Halsey Company, George M. Miller, chairman, Thomas M. Bancroft, chairman, Executive Committee, and George H. Lanier, Jr., president. The firm's activities over the years have widely expanded to include not only ducks and heavy cottons but drills, twills, industrial fabrics, work-clothing fabrics, synthetic fabrics and woolen and worsted goods.

J. W. VALENTINE CO. INC. began business at 40 Worth Street under that name in 1935. The firm was an outgrowth of some of the principals of Haywood, Mackay and Valentine, Inc., founded five years earlier. Mr. Joseph W. Valentine and Mr. Edward R. Valentine had been with The Farish Company until 1926, at which time they joined the T. Holt Haywood Department of Frederick Vietor & Achelis. This illustrates how Worth Street continuously renews itself, training its leaders within itself. J. W. Valentine Co. Inc. is one of the most recently formed large selling houses, but its personnel goes back far in the Street history—a living example of the proverb, "The more things change, the more they remain the same."

J. W. Valentine Co. Inc. were among the first to stress development of synthetic fibers in fabric trends. They were the first to tell the textile story over the radio in their public-service program "Textile Topics," and to realize the value of industry-wide public relations.

There are many other important primary market firms in the Worth Street District—firms who handle the sale of goods for the mills. Many of these firms have long records of accomplishments. While some of these firms are not as old as some of the earlier firms who have made Worth Street history, still they are all writing the history of the Street for tomorrow.

Spartan Mills, Inc., William Whitman Company, Inc., Wilson and Bradbury Sales Corp., Springs Mills, Inc., The Dunson Sales Company, Neisler Mills Co., Inc., Southern Textile Commission Co., Inc., Tripp, Kory & Co., W. S. Libbey Company, Clinton Cottons, Inc., Chatham Manufacturing Co., and Dundee Mills, Inc., are all a credit to the textile industry.

The history of Worth Street has also been written by many fine firms who buy the products of the mills and who are active in the Street. A number of brokers have played, and play, an important part in the daily distribution of the products of the mills through Worth Street. Converting firms, large and small, along with the finishing plants, have used their ingenuity to create more attractive goods for the consuming public.

Wholesalers have followed many and varied plans for placing the products in the hands of retailers throughout the nation. Buying offices have performed a valuable service to the Street —men with experience who know their markets and have from time to time been of inestimable service in working out market problems for the benefit of all. It has taken, and still takes, all of these components to make Worth Street the textile capital of the world.

CHAPTER XXVII

The Clubs and Associations of Worth

The Arkwright Club and the Merchants Club are as much a part of the history of the village of Worth as its businesses and buildings. These clubs are entwined with the business and social activity of Worth Street.

The older of the two, the Merchants Club, began its career in 1871 at 106-108 Leonard Street, and is spoken of today as the oldest luncheon club in continuous operation in New York City. The first Board of Directors, as chosen in 1872, was made up of:

Henry F. Spaulding	Gilbert L. Beeckman
Edward M. Townsend	Stewart L. Woodford
William Turnbull	Cornelius N. Bliss
Furman Hunt	Henry A. Page
Samuel Keyser	William L. Pomeroy
William T. Garner	William Post
Hewlett Scudder	William H. Stewart
James M. Dunbar	Samuel B. Dana

The first officers elected by the Board were: Henry F. Spaulding, president; William Turnbull, vice president; Hewlett Scudder, treasurer, and Cornelius N. Bliss, secretary.

When the imposing New York Life Insurance Company Building was erected at the corner of Leonard Street and Broadway, the club moved to magnificent quarters there in 1893 and remained until 1941. It then moved to 26 Thomas Street, where it now owns its own home. Its present membership is limited to 450 resident members, most of whom are

151

associated with the textile industry. The Merchants Club, with its own home, actively reflects the desires and wishes of those in the district for a permanent textile village—a village that will always be a great credit to a great industry.

On the stair of this club is now found a famous painting, popularly known as "Sell and Repent." The picture is of one John Preston of England, a merchant dealer in wool and yarns. A legend says that in his daily dealings he often remarked, when an order was available, that he would "sell and regret later," or "sell and regret," or "I'll sell if I repent." This painting was given to the club by W. B. Fullerton. Under it one may read: "This is a portrait of John Preston, Merchant, Bradford, England, who, about 1788 coined the phrase 'Sell and Repent.' "

The Arkwright Club was organized in 1893, when the following members and directors applied for a charter:

George H. Frieze	William Thayer Shedd
John O'Sullivan	Edward S. Bowland
George O. Leavitt	Frank Cabot
William W. Marston	William C. Engle
Robert Rhodes	Henry B. Keen
William T. West	Frederick William Gwinn
Henry G. Woodruff	William H. Allen
Frank D. Ward	

The club was first located at the southwest corner of Duane Street and Broadway. About 1896 the building at 320 Broadway was erected, and the two top floors were reserved for the Arkwright Club. This gave it an attractive new home. The view was excellent, and the members not only could see the Hudson River and the Jersey shore but could also scan the Worth Street District. In the old records of the club there is a reference to "securing new draperies for the ladies' smoking room." Some will wonder why the ladies had a special smoking room fifty years ago, but the records of the House Committee seem to prove it. In 1938 the club moved to larger and even finer quarters at 40 Worth Street, where it is conveniently located on the fifteenth floor. The club, named for Richard Arkwright, the great inventor of textile machinery, has about 1,000 members.

Since textiles have been sold on Worth Street for one hundred years, Worthsonians have an understanding of co-operation. When one first goes into a business he is usually preoccupied with the business and is inclined to resent the intrusion of competitors. In time, however, knowledge and wisdom are gained, and competitors find they have something in common, something they can share, which will make business more pleasant even though still competitive.

They soon find there are some things about a market place which the individual working alone cannot accomplish, but which competitors working together can achieve. When this happens the competitors get together and form an association for their common good.

Textile trade associations first arose among the mills, and were relatively late in being formed in the market place. The manufacturers found it easy to exchange information on how to card and spin their yarn and weave their cloth, for each had his problems. So the National Association of Cotton Manufacturers was formed almost a century ago, and the American Cotton Manufacturers Association traces its ancestry back into the nineteenth century.

In the market place, however, each seller was for a long time suspicious of his competitors. It took some earth-shaking developments to throw marketmen together to deal with a common problem, and the growth of modern merchandising methods has kept this cooperative spirit alive among them.

Early experiments in cooperation go back to the years just before World War I. At that time people in the gingham business—a tremendous business in the days before modern textile printing—found that they had some joint problems bigger than any individual could handle. The cotton duck people also got together and formed the Cotton Duck Association. There were also some men's shirting problems that lent themselves to cooperation.

Perhaps the most significant cooperative development was precipitated during World War I, when growing military needs for cotton textiles resulted in the formation, on June 17, 1918, of the Association of Cotton Textile Merchants of New York. Sellers banded together to see that the military was supplied in France. Later the Association came to the rescue of the government and industry in seeing that postwar surpluses were successfully liquidated without damage to the dry goods market generally. The same organization performed a like task, but on a far greater scale, during World War II, and again rallied to the colors in the tight situation faced by industry and government in the early stages of the Korean War.

Many are the problems that can be met by a trade association which could not be solved by the members working as individuals. The problem may be one such as the codified Worth Street Rules, with the Standard Salesnote. This problem was solved by buyers and sellers working cooperatively through some thirteen trade organizations. Or the problem may be one of taxation, or one of quality standards in merchandise, or one of fair trade practices—anything from mobilizing an industry for war down to securing police protection against a wave of burglaries. The Association of Textile Merchants has done all these jobs, and thousands of others, for the primary market place.

Worth Street has many other trade groups. The Textile Fabrics Association is the watchdog for the important converting industry centered in New York. The National Association of Finishers of Textile Fabrics looks out for the problems of the finishers. The Wholesale Dry Goods Institute constantly reminds the world of the importance of wholesaling in textile distribution. The Textile Export Association of the United States, an outgrowth of the Association of Cotton-Textile Merchants and the old Cotton Textile Institute, solves the problems of foreign commerce. The American Cotton Manufacturers Institute, leading mill organization, has an office in the district, as has also the National Cotton Council.

The textile trade associations in Worth Street provide a particularly valuable link, since on the one hand they are part of the market place while on the other they deal with the problems of fibers, of mills, of distribution and of consumer groups. Each association has its work cut out for it, as a specialist in its field, and through these associations business firms with common problems are banded together. The various groups can in this way work harmoniously to solve problems for the general good of the industry at large.

Worth Street, Inc. has recently been organized as a civic association to promote the welfare of the district by those who are interested in its future. It has great possibilities for good, and will eventually serve the community well with some coordinated planning.

The Worth Street Historical Society has been organized with the announced purpose of preserving the old records of the historic center, and of setting up a Textile Museum to display and preserve fabrics, trademarks, machinery, clothing and any other items of textile interest in general.

The Worth Street area, when it was the ancient Indian capital of Manahatta, flew the first flag or emblem on Manhattan Island. While the Manhattan Indians had no flag as flags are made today, still they did have an emblem which they respected—the ceremonial tomahawk of the sachem, bedecked with thongs or streamers in bright colors, which, when waved on high, led them into battle and gave them a symbol around which to rally.

The village of Worth in its long career has lived under many flags—in fact, more flags than most other centers of the world. The first European flag flown in Worth Village was the Tricolor of Holland, which superseded the Indian flag when the Dutch bought the land in 1626. The Union Jack of England followed in 1664, only to be hauled down when the

Dutch Tricolor again flew over the island in 1673 and until the following year, when the British flag returned.

In March 1775 a new flag with a red field, known as the Union Flag, was hoisted on a liberty pole on the Common not far from Worth Street by the Liberty Boys. There is little doubt that it was also flown at the time from the buildings or the grounds of the new hospital. In January 1776 the first colonial flag, the "Great Union Flag," was flown over Washington's Army near Boston, and one can imagine the new hospital again rushing to hoist the new colors.

On July 9, 1776, General Washington officially raised this Colonial Flag on Manhattan Island when he read the Declaration of Independence before his assembled troops. But by September the British Army had returned. The Union Jack again flew over Worth Street when the British took over the hospital, and used it for several years—in fact, until they evacuated the island in 1783. In 1777, the Flag of the Thirteen States was adopted by the American Congress, but the British were in possession of the hospital at that time and kept the Union Jack flying.

In 1795 the new nation adopted a new flag of fifteen stripes, alternating red and white, and fifteen stars in a field of blue, which undoubtedly flew from the flagpole of the tall center building of the hospital. This same flag flew over the hospital and over many other buildings during the War of 1812 in the Worth Street area. In 1818 Congress provided that the flag should consist of thirteen horizontal stripes alternating red and white, with a Union of twenty white stars in a blue field. Since that day, no flag other than the Stars and Stripes has flown over the Worth Street area, except as a courtesy to visitors or in connection with some important celebration.

On every national holiday, Worth Street breaks out a row of American flags to be sure that no one forgets. In fact, the parade of flags has become a tradition in the Street, which boasts a total of eighty-four flagpoles. No one knows which firm flew the first flag on Worth Street after it became a textile center, but this old tradition has continued down to the present day.

During the War of 1812, many flags waved brightly from the fine residences in the area. The cloth for these flags was being handled by the textile firms then located near the tip of the island. Some of the cloth was imported, and some made on the hand looms of the day. The Street in its long career has made millions of yards of fabric for American flags.

Worth Street now has an historic flag of its own, an emblem of the first inhabited spot on Manhattan Island—a flag it can fly with pride along with the National Emblem.

Chapter XXVIII

The Banks of Worth

The Village of Worth is also a banking center of much renown. It is not surprising that such banks as The Chase National Bank, the Chemical Bank and Trust Co. and The Hanover Bank established branches in the Worth Street center, nor that within the wider area of the Village of Worth there are branches of the National City Bank and the Manufacturers Trust Company near Canal Street and the East River Savings Bank near Reade Street, for the first bank on Manhattan Island was established in the Worth Street area a thousand years ago on the present site of the Chemical Bank and Trust Company, now 320 Broadway. It was the "Manahatta Wampum Bank," owned by the Manhattes Tribe. On that site the Indians made wampum, the money of their day, and did such banking as was needed at the time. Their wampum represented a definite value, for even the Dutch used it on Manhattan for several years as a medium of exchange.

The first American bank on Manhattan was a branch bank of the United States, but the next followed shortly when the Bank of New York was organized in 1784 by Alexander Hamilton; while the third was the Manhattan Company set up in 1799 by Aaron Burr.

Today, there are about 15,000 banks in the United States, but the financial center of America is still on Manhattan Island not a mile from the site of the old Manahatta Wampum Bank.

THE CHASE NATIONAL BANK

The Chase National Bank through one of its components can trace its history in New York back for 143 years, inasmuch as the old Mechanics Bank, which later became the Mechanics & Metals National Bank, was chartered in 1810. However,

158

the Chase, named for Salmon P. Chase, Secretary of the Treasury in Lincoln's Cabinet, expanded rapidly after its establishment in 1877, and experienced an accelerated growth in the decade beginning 1920 through a series of consolidations with other banks. It was through these mergers that the bank's two branches in the Worth Street District were acquired.

The Importers and Traders branch at the corner of Worth and Church Streets inherits its name from the old Importers and Traders Bank. In 1908 it moved to 247 Broadway and in 1923 was merged with the Equitable Trust Company. In 1928, the branch secured its present quarters in the 40 Worth Street Building. Two years later, the Equitable Trust Company was merged with The Chase National Bank.

Chase's Worth Street branch, formerly a branch of the Mechanics & Metals National Bank (which was merged with Chase in 1926), was in 1906 the Lispenard branch of the Lincoln Trust Company, but later moved to the New York Life Building at the corner of Broadway and Leonard Street, becoming the Leonard Street branch. In 1922 Lincoln Trust was merged with Mechanics & Metals, and in March 1925 quarters were obtained in the present building, 335 Broadway, at Worth Street, and the branch was again renamed—this time as the Worth Street Branch.

The mergers and consolidations which have created the present Chase National Bank tell an interesting historical story.

(Year of organization of merged banks shown in parentheses)

    I. METROPOLITAN BANK (1851): November 23, 1921

        a. Maiden Lane National Bank (1904): May 1, 1905

        b. National Shoe & Leather Bank (successor to Shoe & Leather Bank organized in 1852): May 1, 1906

        c. Hamilton Trust Company (1891): January 29, 1921

160   TOMAHAWKS TO TEXTILES

II. Mechanics and Metals National Bank (successor to Mechanics Bank, organized in 1810): April 12, 1926

    a. Leather Manufacturers National Bank (successor to Leather Manufacturers Bank, organized in 1832): April 16, 1904

    b. National Copper Bank (1907): January 29, 1910

    c. Fourth National Bank (1864): June 18, 1914

    d. New York Produce Exchange Bank (1883): June 21, 1920

    e. Lincoln Trust Company (1902): June 24, 1922

III. Mutual Bank (1890): December 28, 1927

IV. Garfield National Bank (organized 1881 as successor to Island City Bank organized 1875 as successor to Ninth Ward Bank organized 1870): January 26, 1929

V. National Park Bank (successor to Park Bank organized in 1856): August 26, 1929

    a. Wells Fargo & Company Bank (1852): March 11, 1911

VI. Interstate Trust Company (1926): June 2, 1930

    a. Franklin National Bank (1923): June 30, 1927

    b. Bloomingdale Brothers, Private Bankers (1914): June 30, 1927

    c. Hamilton National Bank (1923): January 21, 1928

    d. Century Bank (Opened January 26, 1920 under name of Slavonic Emigrant Bank;

changed March 2, 1925 to Century
Bank): August 10, 1929
> 1. Dewey State Bank (1926): Jan-
> uary 16, 1928

VII. EQUITABLE TRUST COMPANY (1902): June 2,
1930
> a. Bowling Green Trust Company (1898):
> March 31, 1909
> b. Madison Trust Company (1902): June 1,
> 1911
> c. Trust Company of America (organized
> 1905 as successor to trust companies 1,
> 2, & 3, below): February 24, 1912
>> 1. North American Trust Company
>> (1896)
>>> a. International Bankers &
>>> Trust Company
>>> (1899): April 26,
>>> 1900
>> 2. City Trust Company (1899)
>> 3. Trust Company of America
>> (1899)
>> 4. Colonial Trust Company (1897):
>> April 26, 1907
> d. Importers & Traders National Bank (1865)
> (successor to Importers & Traders Bank
> organized in 1855): June 29, 1923
> e. Seaboard National Bank (1883): Septem-
> ber 16, 1929
>> 1. Mercantile Trust Company
>> (1917): April 1, 1922
>> 2. New Netherland Bank (1907):
>> February 1, 1928

VIII. AMERICAN EXPRESS BANK & TRUST COMPANY
(1930): December 21, 1931

CHEMICAL BANK & TRUST COMPANY

The Chemical Bank & Trust Company was founded in 1824 as the Chemical Bank, its first office being at 216 Broadway, opposite St. Paul's Chapel. Chemical Bank was established through a legislative amendment to the state charter of the New York Chemical Manufacturing Company which permitted the company to engage in general banking. The president of the Chemical Bank in 1831, John Mason, was made president of the first railroad on Manhattan, the Harlem Railroad, which had its terminus in the Worth Street area.

In 1844, when its twenty-one-year banking charter expired, the New York Chemical Manufacturing Company discontinued its manufacture of "blue vitrol, alum alcohol, tartar emetic, refined camphor, borax, copperas, drugs, medicines, paints and dyer's colors," and the name Chemical Bank was adopted, under which the institution confined its business to banking.

A full banking charter was procured, and in the early part of 1850 the office was moved to larger quarters at 270 Broadway, near Chambers Street, where it was located in the heart of the wholesale textile market, which then centered between Cedar and Chambers Streets.

From this location the Chemical Bank continued to serve the expanding textile industry after it moved to the Worth Street area only a few blocks north.

On June 3, 1864, the Chemical became a national bank, and in 1865 changed its name to the Chemical National Bank. In 1914 it became a member of the Federal Reserve System, and continued as a national bank until May 1929, when it reverted to its original status as a state-chartered institution, changing its corporate title to the Chemical Bank & Trust Company and retaining its membership in the Federal Reserve.

The Citizens National Bank was organized in 1851 at 401 Broadway, and the Ninth National Bank in 1864 at 407

Broadway. These two banks merged in 1901 with headquarters at 401 Broadway. The Central National Bank was organized in 1864 at 320 Broadway and in 1904 this Bank merged with the Citizens National—the home of the combined banks being at 320 Broadway. In 1920 Chemical acquired the Citizens National Bank and it was consolidated with the main office at 270 Broadway. In 1928 Chemical reopened the office at 320 Broadway to serve the Worth Street area. The United States Mortgage and Trust Company merged with Chemical in 1929, to be followed by the Continental Bank and Trust Company in 1948, and the National Safety Bank and Trust Company of New York in 1951. Since 1928 Chemical's main office has been at 165 Broadway.

Because of its policy of maintaining gold redemption throughout the financial panics during the latter half of the nineteenth century, Chemical won for itself the name of "Old Bullion."

THE HANOVER BANK

When a group of businessmen met at Hanover Square in 1851, to plan a bank, they decided at first to call it "the Bank of Hanover Square," but a few days later the name was shortened to The Hanover Bank. After more than a century this is still the name of the bank, although there have been changes from time to time.

When this bank was formed, New York City was experiencing a rapid growth. Its population was about one-half million, including 200,000 recently arrived immigrants. And yet there were farms and pasture lands above 14th Street. Six years later the country suffered a reaction from the Gold Boom of '49, twelve hundred commercial houses failing in New York alone. By 1860 the storm had passed, but the country was faced by the impending War Between the States. The Hanover Bank lived through these times.

In the years that followed, the Hanover greatly expanded its facilities through mergers and absorptions. In 1901 the

Hanover absorbed the Continental Bank, which had been founded in 1853. Then in 1912 the Hanover and the Gallatin National Bank (formerly the National Bank, established in 1831) merged. The Greenwich Bank (established in 1831) and the Hanover merged in 1927 to form the Hanover National Bank of the City of New York.

In 1911 the Union Trust Company (established in 1865) absorbed the Plaza Bank, which dated back to 1831. Then in 1918 the Union Trust Company and the Central Union Trust Company (which had been established in 1873) merged into the Central Union Trust Company of New York.

In 1929 the Central Union Trust Company and the Hanover National Bank of the City of New York merged to form the Central Hanover Bank & Trust Company. This finally became The Hanover Bank again.

Chapter XXIX

The Journals of Worth

Worth Street and the Fourth Estate have had a great deal in common over the years, and the Street and the newspapers that serve it are mutually indebted. This is particularly true of the so-called trade press as distinguished from the regular daily newspapers. Two such daily trade papers supply Worth Street every morning with market information, price quotations, news affecting business from all quarters of the globe, and a grist of data on products and distribution and people. The New York *Journal of Commerce,* which was founded by a textile man, goes back some 126 unbroken years, and the *Daily News Record* has a history of 61 years. Since newspapers usually are preoccupied with telling stories about other people, it may not be averse to tell a bit of a story about the newspapers.

In the case of the *Journal of Commerce,* it should be noted that it was first published on September 1, 1827, and except for the *Evening Post* earlier established by Alexander Hamilton is the oldest newspaper in publication in New York. This paper in 1840 absorbed the *Daily Gazette,* and so by collateral descent goes back to November 17, 1783, when the *Gazette,* originally the *Independent Journal or General Advertiser,* first hit the streets, proclaiming the evacuation of the last British troops from American soil. So measured, the *Journal of Commerce* is New York's oldest newspaper. Only papers in Philadelphia and Charleston, South Carolina, can look further into the past. The *Independent Journal* was a tabloid newspaper rather than a full-page-format paper such as the

165

Journal of Commerce is; the *Daily News Record* started con-
version to tabloid size in 1926.

The founders of the *Journal of Commerce* were Arthur
Tappan, a merchant in silk and textiles, one of whose earlier
associates helped found the Catlin textile firm about eight
years later, and Samuel Finley Breese Morse, inventor of the
telegraph. It was first issued from the Merchants Exchange,
Wall Street, then the city's finest business building. In latter
years it was at 32 Broadway, when it maintained a separate
textile office at 54 Worth Street. Later it was at 46 Barclay
Street, since torn down to make way for the new federal building and post office which the Navy calls the "U.S.S. 90
Church," and in the Pulitzer Building in Park Row, home of
the old New York *World,* the once golden-domed edifice now
coming down to make traffic clover leaves at the approaches to
Brooklyn Bridge. Just this year the owners of the *Journal of
Commerce* seem to have concluded that the experiment of
126 years ago might last, for they have finally bought a building of their own in Varick Street.

The *Journal of Commerce* was originally concerned with
public morals. In fact, Morse became upset by a little French
lady, Mme. Francisque Hutin, then appearing in a Bowery
music hall, and wrote Tappan a 2750-word letter about the
need for a newspaper which would halt such nonsense. Tappan
put $30,000 into this plot, and the *Journal of Commerce* re-
sulted. But Mme. Hutin continued to delight her audiences
until 1832. It is said Tappan, who was making money in silk,
had no thought of profiting from his paper and, in fact, lost
money on it. In other words, here was a publisher who sub-
scribed to the old reportorial dictum that in newspaper work
"you don't make any money but you have a lot of fun."

The *Journal of Commerce* is known to have missed publication but twice. Its office was burned out in the great fire of
1835. Later, sympathetic to the Southern cause, it was seized
and briefly shut down by a squad of Union troops on orders
of President Abraham Lincoln during the Civil War.

The *Daily News Record,* formerly the *Daily Trade Record,* is part of the monumental newspaper achievement known as Fairchild Publications, from the Fairchild family, its originators and owners. It started in Chicago in 1892 as a textile, clothing and credit paper, and promptly moved to New York, to the center of the textile industries. Here it arose to challenge the hegemony of the *Journal of Commerce* in textile news reporting; the rivalry between the two has been sometimes white-hot and sometimes quiescent. The *Record* has proliferated into a lengthy list of daily, weekly, and monthly publications, mostly in the textile and apparel fields.

Personalities are difficult to discuss in this competitive field, but in connection with the older paper the name of the late John J. Manning, its textile editor for many years, is outstanding. John Manning came from the Fall River and New Bedford textile area to news reporting in New York, and on the *Sun* covered the famous fashion competition between the great E. Berry Wall, "King of the Dudes," and the actor Robert Hilliard. He covered the Lizzie Borden murder case, the first widely publicized murder trial over the then new network of the Associated Press, which he had a part in founding. His imprint on Worth Street is still remembered by many merchants. As to the younger paper, its leaders are still largely about and must fall to the appraisal of future historians. However, no name can possibly be brighter in the *Daily News Record* hierarchy, past, present or future, than that of its editor of many years, Harry Riemer.

There are innumerable textile-newspaper stories that might be told, but one will suffice. Years ago, a well-known textile finishing company developed a new waterproof finish, and to advertise it put live ducks in crates and sent them by express to clients. Crates of ducks went to the textile trade papers also, and in a certain paper one was duly received and stowed alongside a desk in the textile department. At this stage an advertising salesman, well fortified with martinis, arrived, looked, pointed, and said, "Is that a duck?" The duck thrust its head through the crate and quacked, but the editor just commented, "The only ducks we know about here are cotton ducks." The salesman polled the surrounding reporters, each of whom responded only "What duck?" or "What have you been drinking?" The bewildered salesman, rubbing his eyes, retreated, and gave up his martinis for a long, long time.

Newspaper coverage of the Worth Street market has changed from the bad old days, which are not so old but that many people remember them. It didn't take long for the rival trade papers to sell subscriptions to the merchants; it took longer to sell them to all the thousands of customers—and in a newspaper, news makes circulation, and circulation makes advertising, and advertising makes money necessary to pay the printers and pressmen, if not support the rest of the organization in luxury. At some stages the paper with the lowest gray-cloth quotations was best liked by the buyers, who could use those printed values to get their goods more cheaply.

Old-time editors and reporters often knew as much as anybody else about stocks and unfilled orders. When stocks of cloth or yarn became unwieldy, it was not then considered unethical, but rather a favor to the market as a whole, to pull the plug by spreading the story that somebody had broken the market an eighth and sold a million yards. Some merchants in these same old days were not beyond joining in this game, for when the debacle was over they would have been the first to sell, and the last man's mills would be in the market for a new sales agency.

The procedure was, of course, not a one-way street. There were times when old-time merchants and old-time newspapermen alike could "bull" the market, to the vast discomfiture of the customers. Over a period of time the score was probably tied. Today's textile papers would tolerate no such shenanigans. Today's merchants have more facts at their elbows, Worth Street is not the "rumor factory" it once was, and today's customers and merchants are more prone to get together on their problems than to throw up the barricades and battle each other into extinction.

Worth Street also is served by the *Worth Street Forecast*, which is published at 64 Worth Street every two weeks, and by numerous other publications. The regular New York dailies, the *Times, Herald-Tribune, Journal-American, World-Telegram & Sun, Daily News, Daily Mirror, Post*, and *Brooklyn Eagle*, all watch the news there, as do press services and papers over an important area of the country, particularly the textile states. There are a score of monthly magazines and other periodicals on textiles. *America's Textile Reporter* of Boston gets a special accolade for its annual Worth Street Edition. Even *Fortune* magazine has devoted the better part of an edition to the Street. *Southern Textile News, Textile World, Textile Age, Textile Industries*, and *Linens and Domestics* are cited, and only the limitations of this volume prevent a longer and equally deserving roster of other members of the press that serves Worth Street—the press Worth Street serves.

CHAPTER XXX

Textiles and America

The story of textiles is the story of a nation and its people, their struggles and their works and their dreams, a combination at once of the prosaic and the unusual, the humdrum and the heroic, joined daily in a long, upward progress. As America is at once the story of the frontiersman and the atom scientist, so is the textile story compounded of the butternut-dyed homespun of the settler and of new fabrics bought in the Village of Worth which go into the making of the atom bomb or which parachute it over the target.

Textiles marked the opening of the factory age as the child of the Industrial Revolution, perhaps its eldest offspring, for textile production and early metal working were the beginning of that massive change in man's affairs. In textiles are found the whole evolution of trade, from the first plant that had to reach out for markets beyond the local community to today's textile marketing mechanism, than which economists admit there is none more complex nor unusual in variety of products or methods of sale.

Textiles have paced the building of American industry: the rise of New England from an area of rock-strewn farms to one of early pre-eminence in the manufacturing arts; the founding of the Southern cotton kingdom and the wool empire of the western ranges and the ocean trade in cotton and wool, silk and sisal, hemp and henequen, flax and burlap. Textiles have led in the regeneration of the South from agricultural dependency to a leading place in the development of new industries. Textiles in the twentieth century have seen new miracles of fibers made from the pulp of the forests and from such strange materials as coal and air and sand.

Villages and towns and cities have been carved out of virgin wilderness, or expanded from the smallest beginnings by the coming of the textile industry. Detroit may spell automobiles, and Pittsburgh steel, but consider the vast range of national upbuilding from textiles. First in the East such textile centers as Lowell and Manchester, New Bedford and Fall River, Lawrence, Lewiston, Biddeford, Providence, and literally scores of other cities and towns—for few were the Eastern centers not so affected—were early touched by the wealth-giving wand of cotton and wool manufacturing.

Consider also such cities as Paterson, pre-eminent in silk weaving; Pennsylvania and New Jersey and other Middle Atlantic States areas still broadly active in textiles; carpet mills in Yonkers and Thompsonville, Amsterdam and Philadelphia; knitting plants spread far and wide.

And finally there is the vast Southern textile area comprising 80 per cent of the spindles on cotton and related fibers, the "mill-a-mile" along the Southern Railway in the southeast, cities and towns stretching in a wide arc from Virginia to Texas, vastly expanded or called into being by the coming of textile manufacturing—centers such as Danville, Greenville, Spartanburg, Greensboro, Burlington, Columbia, Atlanta, Macon, Newnan, and Sylacauga.

Textiles are not made in a few big centers and there are no single dominant companies. More than 3,500 plants make textiles in America today—from cotton, wool, rayon and other fibers—all the way from Maine to Texas. Untold thousands of factories from San Francisco to Seventh Avenue, New York, and beyond fashion them into garments and other useful things. Mercantile establishments everywhere, wholesale and retail, bring the final products to Americans and to customers beyond its borders and seas.

One and one-half million Americans grow cotton in the South. Half a million are engaged in wool growing, covering every state in the nation. More than 1,000,000 Americans work in textile plants. More than 1,300,000 work in the apparel trades. Untold numbers do the banking and transporting and storing and wholesaling and retailing and other tasks involved. Line up any ten employed Americans and there will be one whose living, directly or indirectly, is derived in whole or in part from the ubiquitous enterprises of this tremendous industry. Translate this into the accumulation of history and it is clear that in the 177 years of our national life textiles and the textile fibers have contributed more to America, in employment, in the building of industry, in the creation of cities and towns, in the growth of a nation, and in dollars realized in foreign commerce, than any other industry.

Great and expanding is the prospect for the future of this industry, with new discoveries adding to the wealth of tried and true items of common knowledge. Think of Nylon and the tremendous investment of duPont in this fiber long before the first commercial pound appeared; or Orlon and Dacron; of fibers of glass, of Dynel and other new materials. Think of rayon and acetate, new within a lifetime, today commonplace. Or again of older materials, cotton the sunshine fiber, wool and others. Eighty per cent of textiles used are still cotton, proving its ability to compete, deriving benefits from new finishes and textures. Only a century and a half ago cotton itself was a "miracle fiber" and its performance today in new forms and uses sustains and advances its reputation and demand.

Truly the things textiles do today combine the commonplace with the surprising.

A person standing on the Washington Bridge or at the Lincoln Tunnel might watch the cars go by—America on wheels, pride and symbol of modern industrial accomplishment. Ninety pounds of cotton went into the making of each passing car. But for cotton and rayon we might still be riding on iron wagon rims. The automobile would be virtually an impossibility.

Another, watching the great Fourdrinier machines making paper, might note the web of pulp carried on its way on great "paper maker's dryer felts"—textile products—essential to paper. Or in a bindery one might see books stitched and bound with cotton thread and cloth.

In the oil fields again one looks on strange new forms of industrial processing. Oil seems far from textiles, but there is "oil press duck" and filters of all kinds in this and other industry; filters for milk in Wisconsin and acids in West Virginia. The textile industry makes 3,000 different kinds of filter fabrics.

Brattice cloth is found in mines far below the surface of the earth, and the New Yorker in his commonplace tunnel, the Eighth Avenue subway, might recall having witnessed the wrapping of the outer shell of that tunnel in millions of yards of cotton sheeting as a membrane in its waterproofing.

One may witness ore being moved from Great Lakes docksides to plants far distant on vast conveyor systems, a plan to displace railroad haulage of heavy bulk freight. Thousands of tons of ore and grain and other goods move daily on these seemingly rubber highways, but embedded in the rubber and its source of strength are tons of heavy cotton fabric.

There are concealed and silent gears in one's automobile built out of textiles, and silent gears in the alarm clock which awakens one to a day of new miracles also laminated out of layers of cotton cloth not far different from the cloth in the shirt one wears.

Such are a few—a very few—vignettes illustrating our national and industrial and farm dependence on textiles, things seldom thought of, such as cotton in the telephone and electric wiring, the fan belt and the vacuum cleaner, the tent over the tobacco field, the binder twine in the harvesting machine in the wheat fields of the West. They are produced by these widely spread textile plants, and flow in an unending river of billions of yards annually through the sales mechanism centered in the Village of Worth.

There are in addition those wartime items, the 10,000 products of the textile industry which the Quartermaster bought for

the winning of World War II—uniforms, overcoats, underwear, bandoliers, gun covers, powder bags, machine gun belts,
rubber boats, surgical goods on which our national life depended.

And they are in addition to the commonplace items, but
even these, to the uninitiate, may be new and strange. Food,
clothing and shelter are life necessities. Of these, clothing is
the responsibility of textiles. But in our complex society these
basic essentials are taken for granted and the bulk of our economy is concerned with goods beyond the essentials. Here too
the mercantile skills of the Village of Worth come fully into
play.

In clothing one must first have clothes to work in, and then
something for "Sunday best." From such bare necessities all
the elements of style and fashion take over, whether in high
style products of American and Parisian designers, or the de-
mocratized versions of fashion for the masses which make
Americans the best dressed people in the world, or sports or
spectator wear, or the informal leisure apparel so much demanded today, or back again full circle to work clothing where
new designs, uniforms, or functional garments meet the needs
of people always desiring that which is new and better.

It goes far from just covering our bodies. Forty per cent
or so of textiles are used for apparel, but the great bulk of it
goes beyond conforming to the law and into a true clothes-
consciousness. Worth Street fosters this interest even as the
television salesman seeks to sell his product, which is an ap-
purtenance of civilization, not a necessity of life. Perhaps 20
per cent more goes into household uses. It is interesting to
speculate how many pounds of textiles are in an American
home: shirts, dresses, underwear, hosiery, outerwear, sheets,
towels, draperies, upholstery, rugs, curtains, and a host of other
visible things, plus invisible electrical insulation, thermal insulation in the walls, and a host of other items.

The remaining 40 per cent are the "industrial items," the
unusual and un-thought-of things that keep American industry

and agriculture in business. Even omitting clothing for the worker, there is hardly an industry in America that does not use textiles in some form, consuming them in the process of making other things as in machine belting and buffing and polishing fabrics, or incorporating them invisibly in their products as the textiles in an automobile tire, or visibly as in the top of a convertible, or the tarpaulin on a truck or over a ship's hatch, or the bag or container or gummed sealing tape used in the shipment of all kinds of farm and factory products.

In the world of commerce are many highways, not all ribbons of concrete or steel. Quite as important are the highways of communication, by telephone, by telegraph, by the personal contact of sales people and production people and people thinking of new products, new uses, new ways of doing things, or again interested in the very commonplace items of everyday life. All of these highways of commercial communication for virtually all of the industries of America as well as the garment and household goods trades converge in the fabulous Village of Worth.

Here is the central clearing house of the great textile industry, a center of renowned textile pioneering of the past and of new pioneering in new fields today, a place where the products and potentials of the nation's mills come together, in the selling function, for marketing to every person in America (for none lives without textiles), to nearly every important industry and enterprise in America, and to many beyond our borders. The tradition is there alongside the new and enterprising vista of the future, the commonplace alongside the strange, the ordinary alongside the astounding. The Village of Worth is a pattern of America at work, and the scale is far from miniature.

CHAPTER XXXI

Worth Street—a Symbol

The name Worth Street today is synonymous with textiles throughout the world. It has come to mean more than a street or locality in New York City: it stands for the men and firms, mills and their products, fibers and fabrics. Worth Street is the symbol of a great industry.

The street itself presents an interesting picture of America. Although only eight blocks long, it crowds four distinct centers into that short space. Broadway divides it into main divisions east and west. The five blocks to the east of Broadway make up Foley Square, the civic center with large government buildings belonging to the city, county and state. At the eastern end is Chatham Square, an apartment, business and church center with its famous Chinatown. At the western end of the street is the Western Union building, a center of communication. Worth Street west of Broadway for two blocks is the great textile center of the world. The Worth Street so well known in the commercial world is the locality around these two blocks, the hub of Worth Village. Not many streets of this length can boast of so much concentrated activity in various fields.

Those who each day work in Worth Street, handling the products of hundreds of textile mills, and the many others who daily communicate with the Street from all parts of the nation and world either as buyers or sellers, sometimes forget the history involved—a history going back not hundreds but thousands of years.

Worth Village, surrounding Worth Street, is truly the historical center of Manhattan, because history in Manhattan began there. Those who now thrive in Worth Village, the site of the village of Manahatta—the Indian capital of the canoe-shaped island Manhattan—are proud of their special heritage. They will agree with those who inhabit the rest of the island that Manhattan is the center of the world. Viewed objectively, these Manhattanites may seem a peculiar people. They settled upon a rock-bound island, thirsted for fresh water for two centuries, burrowed deep holes in the rocky surface, honeycombed the rocky foundations with great tunnels, pushed enormous buildings up to the skies, and filled in the shore line to create more living room.

But before all this the original inhabitants, the Indians of Manahatta, upon the site of which Worth Village now stands, lived an ideal existence. They had an ample supply of fresh water from a lake. The sea and land supplied their needs for food and clothing. The coming of Hudson put an end to this. The men who followed him were restless traders and men of business, not content to idle their lives away.

Today in the village of Worth is found the close association of friends and neighbors, with an interest in one another, that is found in communities throughout America.

The confidence with which people throughout the world buy American textile products has its real foundation in Worth Street. The reliance that the consumer places in a local merchant depends upon a long chain of responsibilities built upon the ideals of the village of Worth. The integrity and character of Worth Street has put a stamp of approval on textiles in general that is recognized by wholesalers and retailers who serve the consumer directly.

The village of Worth is not only the historical center of Manhattan and the hub of the textile world; it is a perfect example of an American business community at its best.

(1)

THE STORY IN MAPS

Any map of Manhattan is fascinating, but when a number of old maps are placed together in chronological order they create a dramatic story of their own. These early maps show the progress northward as new streets were laid out. They also reflect the early history of our nation, much of which centered around the island that became the first capital of the United States.

The village of Manahatta was an important place in the Indian world, and the ancient history of Manhattan revolved largely around that village and its beautiful lake, the site of Worth Street's textile village today. The first Dutch settlement, Mannados, later called New Amsterdam, was the first capital of the Dutch colony, and the colonial history of Manhattan in turn revolved around that village at the island's toe.

Because of the narrowness of the island, the Dutch and later the English could expand only northward. But even then the growth was very slow, block by block; houses were built on every available inch of the toe until the increasing population was forced out by sheer weight of numbers. Although the two sites were only one mile apart, it required two hundred years for New Amsterdam to reach the site of old Manahatta.

Over the years many designations have been applied to the area covered in all, or part, by the Village of Worth: Manahatta, Damen Farm, Calch Hook Farm, Kalchhoeck Farm, Rutgers Farm, Rutgers Estate, Lispenard Farm, Hospital Grounds, Freshwater, the Park, the Fishing Grounds, the Marketplace, Textile Center, Worth Street, Worth Street District, the Textile Center of the World. And many are the names that have been applied to the settlement on the toe of the island: Capsie, Capsee, Mannados, New Amsterdam, the Fort, New York, the Tip, the Toe, the Battery. The area between the two centers—the "Mile Expanse"—has at various times been referred to as Manahatta to Capsie, Manahatta to Kapsee, Manahatta to Mannados, New Amsterdam to Manahatta, Bowling Green to Collect, Bowling Green to Fresh Water, Tip to the Pond, Toe to the Canal, and Battery to Worth.

The first known map of Manhattan shows the island as it was supposed to be in 1653. A comparison of this map with others made in succeeding years not only indicates the growth in population but also the increase in area of the island itself as the shore line was filled in.

All the maps in this book are reproduced by courtesy of The New-York Historical Society, New York City, to whom grateful acknowledgment is made.

MAP 1

1653

This map, the earliest available of the Worth Street area, shows the horseshoe in which was located the historic Indian Village of Manahatta, now the location of the Village of Worth. There is no official map of this Manhattes Indian village, for the Indians knew nothing of map-making and cared even less. The Dutch, in turn, made no map of the village when they arrived, but the site of the village is well authenticated.

The Indian village was located on the western shore of Manahatta Lake, marked Collect, and in the primitive forests shown in the horseshoe. In this village, as noted in Chapter IV, was located Manahatta Circle, Manahatta Fort, The Sachama Wicker, Manahatta School, Manahatta Treasury, Manahatta Brewery, the Wigwamtels, the Long Houses and the various things that made up the Indian capital village. The swamps which formed the horseshoe surrounding the village gave it protection from enemies for a thousand years. To the east of the lake is shown more primitive forests. This area was also the Werpoes, or planting ground.

This map clearly shows the outline of the swamp which earlier was the ancient salt-water passage across the Island that created two islands. In 1653 a stream led from the lake to the East River, while from the northern end of the lake another stream passes along to the Hudson River.

Superimposed on this old map are some points of interest in the Dutch era. Kalch-Hoek, the name given to the farm owned by Damen, is shown on the Indian village site. The point of land jutting into the lake, which tended to form two lakes, is also marked Kalch Hoek. The present Worth Street crosses the old lake bed along this point of land.

Just south of the area was the public pasture that extended into the present City Hall Park. On the right was the Dutch windmill of Jan Teunizen. Bowerie Lane was then known as Heerewegh Straat. Near by, Wolfert Weber had a tavern. Broadway ended at the Common, now City Hall Park. Map 2 shows the location of the Indian village site in relation to the first Dutch settlement, New Amsterdam, at the lower end of the Island.

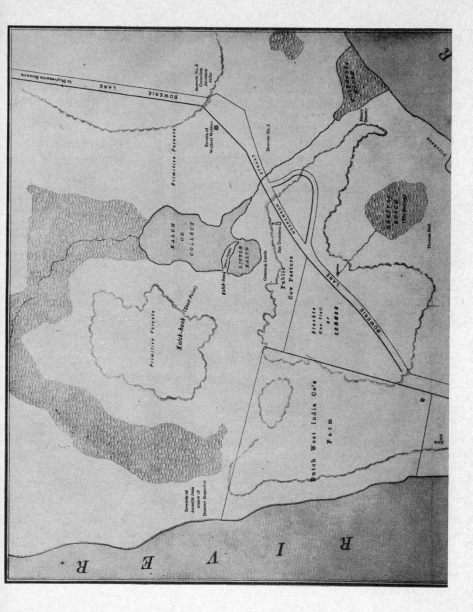

MAP 2

1653. The Lower End of Manhattan Island During
the Dutch Era

This map shows the location of the first white settlement on
the Island. Capsie Rocks is the name given to a large group of
rocks off the tip of the island. The name comes from the small
Indian village which was near by. One of these large rocks, or tiny
islands, became a fort and later an amusement center, Castle
Garden. These rocks are now a part of Manhattan since the space
between them and the shore was filled in. Schreyers Hoek, or
Weepers Point, is at the southern tip of the island.

Fort Amsterdam is shown on the site of the present Custom
House, together with the Governor's House, the Secretary's
House and the Dutch Church. Just north of the Fort was the first
well, and on this map the present Bowling Green Park is called
The Plaine. Broadway is De Heere Straat (Great Highway). At its
lower end Broadway is shown rather close to the Hudson, since
at that time the shore line had not been filled in as shown on
Map Six.

The northern limit of the village was De Wall Straat, along
which is shown the fortified wall with stone forts and gates leading to the countryside to the north. The waterway leading up
Heere Graft (now Broad Street) is still a small stream flowing
in a conduit under the present street.

The locations of many historical sites are shown: Adrian Block
House 1614, first white habitation, first public mill, and many
others.

New Amsterdam was incorporated February 1, 1653, and
this map was made at that time. This year New York is celebrating its 300th anniversary.

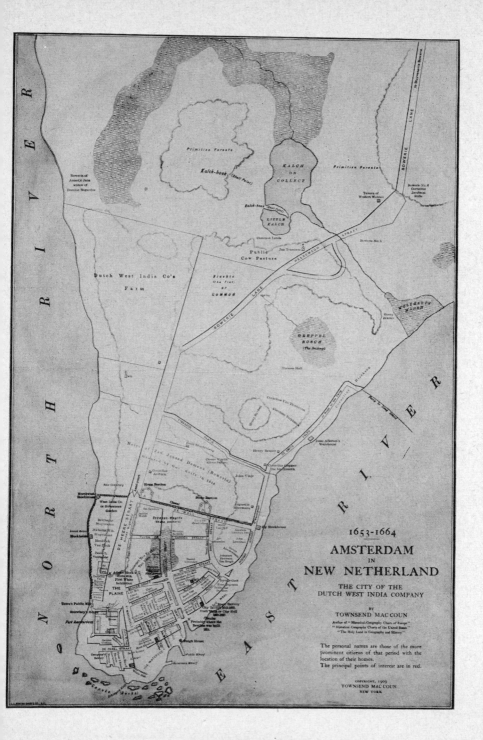

1653-1664

AMSTERDAM
IN
NEW NETHERLAND

THE CITY OF THE
DUTCH WEST INDIA COMPANY

BY
TOWNSEND MAC COUN

Author of "Historical-Geography Charts of Europe"
"Historical-Geography Charts of the United States"
"The Holy Land in Geography and History"

The personal names are those of the more
prominent citizens of that period with the
location of their homes.
The principal points of interest are in red.

COPYRIGHT, 1909
TOWNSEND MAC COUN
NEW YORK

MAP 3

1661. "The Duke's Plan for the Towne of Mannados,
or New Amsterdam"

The first English Map of Manhattan. "Governours Garden" is shown on the Hudson River side of the island, while "Ye Governours House" is on the East River side with the Fort between.

According to the scale shown, the little settlement was about six hundred yards long and on an average of about four hundred yards wide.

The map is not very accurate as to the streets or the waterfront. The Maine Land and Longe Isleland shores are completely out of proportion, as well as the Bay marked "Heads."

The scale reads: "This scale of Five Hundred Yeardes is for the Towne."

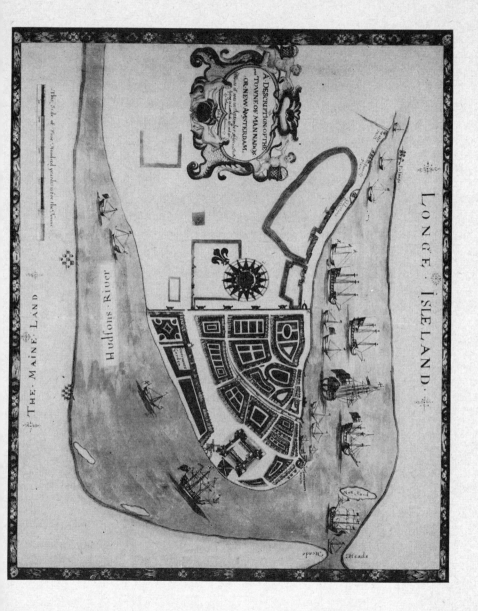

A DESCRIPTION OF THE
TOWNE OF MANNADOS
OR NEW AMSTERDAM.

LONGE · ISLE · LAND ·

THE · MAINE · LAND ·

Hudſons · River

The Scale of Fiue Hundred yeardes is for the Towne

Nut Iland

MAP 4

1730

The Anthony Rutgers Farm had succeeded the Kalch-Hoek Farm. A powder house had been built on Kalch-Hoek between the two lakes. Kalch-Hoek itself had become Collect.

The famous Teawater Pump appears to the southeast of the lakes, and Bowerie Lane had become the Post Road to Boston. The Worth Street area was only a farming section with an old Indian trail, then a country road, leading to it. The Dukes Farm (1664-1674), southwest of the Rutgers Farm, had become in turn Kings Farm (1674-1702), Queen's Farm (1702-1705), and Church Farm when granted to Trinity by Queen Anne in 1705.

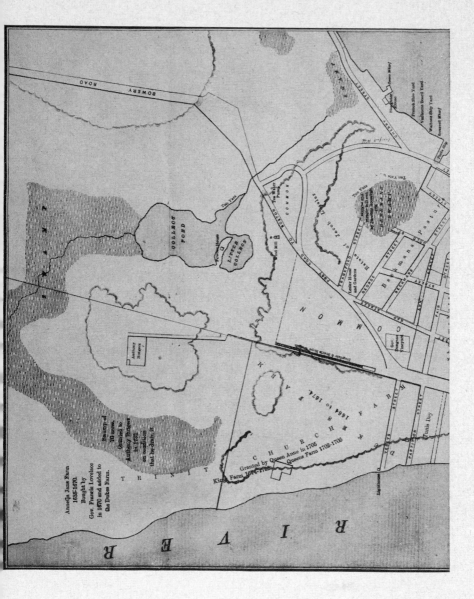

MAP 5

1731. "A Plan of the City of New York from
an actual Survey"

After one hundred years of Dutch and English occupation the city had expanded only six blocks north of Wall
Street.

The route of the present Pearl Street was then known
as Pearl, Dock and Queen Streets. The Common is shown
where the City Hall is now located.

Broadway is shown as Broad Way, and extended only
to the Common. The continuation to the northeast was
known as the High Road to Boston.

What was later Broadway north of the Common was then
a country road up to the Anthony Rutgers Farm, now
Worth Village, and along this road was the Dugdale and
Searles Rope Mill.

Collect Pond is shown at the right, and the Worth Street
area is just west of it under the Seal of the City, which was
placed in the upper right hand corner. The names of some
streets have been changed and new streets added since the
previous map.

The city has now been divided into six wards: South
Ward, Dock Ward, West Ward, East Ward, North Ward
and Montgomerie's Ward.

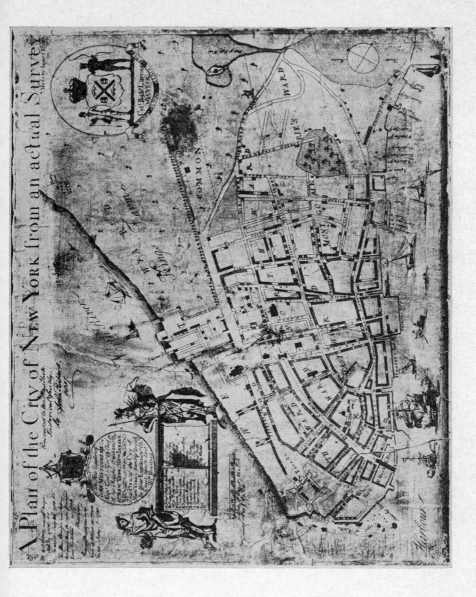

A Plan of the City of New York from an actual Survey

MAP 6

1742

The right half of this map shows the Anthony Rutgers Farm, which is sketched in sections.

The map also shows a section of the so-called palisades or fortified line built across the Island as a protection for the little city to the south against possible attack during the French and Indian War. This line had six blockhouses or forts, one of which was located at Broadway between Chambers and Reade Streets. Much public scandal arose regarding the cost and advisability of this line of fortification. In 1748 the Rutgers Farm became the Lispenard Farm.

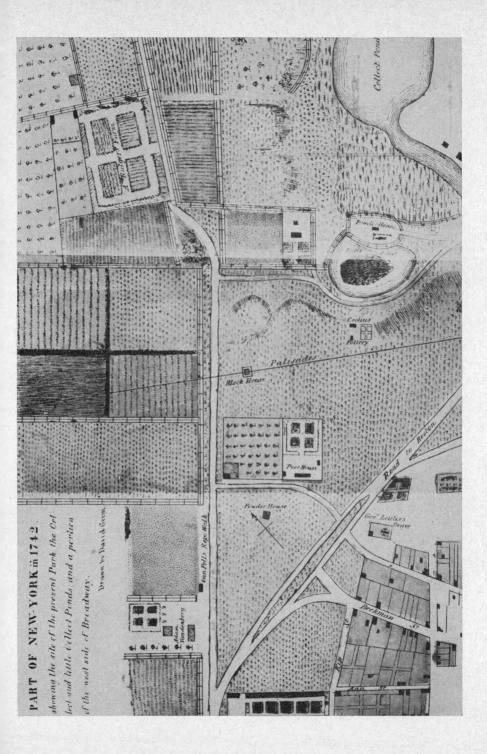

PART OF NEW-YORK in 1742.

showing the site of the present Park the Col
lect and little Collect Ponds: and a portion
of the west side of Broadway.

Drawn by David Grim

MAP 7

1755

This map also shows the line of fortifications. The palisades, or fortified line, had six block houses or forts, marked No. 30, and four gates through the line, marked No. 31. The map also shows the development on the east of the lake around the eastern end of what is now Worth Street and Chatham Square.

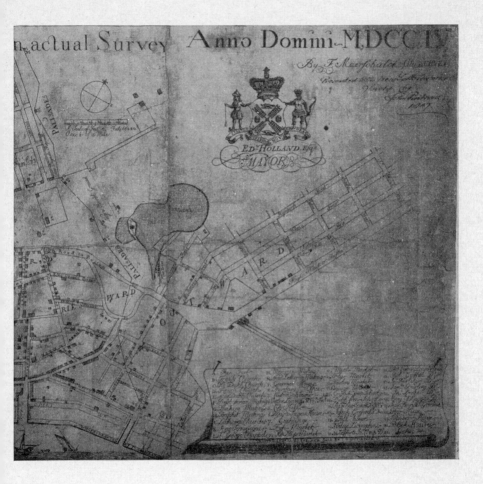

MAP 8

1766

Streets have been laid out up to Chambers Street, and a
few more were laid out to the east of the Worth Street area
along the Bowery, but not many houses had yet been built
in this area.

The Freth Water (Fresh Water) Lake is seen on this
map, as well as the historic horseshoe in which the old
Indian village, later the Anthony Rutgers Farm, was located. The horseshoe was formed by the lakes and swamps.

By this time the old rope mill shown on Broadway on
Map Five had disappeared, and Broadway itself had
reached the present Worth Street area.

Another ward had been added to the city, Out Ward,
covering the area north of the present City Hall.

MAP 9

1766

This shows the Worth Street area in 1766. It is a portion of Map Eight.

Broadway extended up to Duane Street, the last street shown, at which corner was the handsome home of Anthony Rutgers with its gardens, here shown as Ranelagh. Church Street extended only to the gardens. Chapel Street, later West Broadway, extended only to the swampland, which was gradually being drained. In 1760 the Rutgers mansion was opened as a place of amusement known as Ranelagh Gardens.

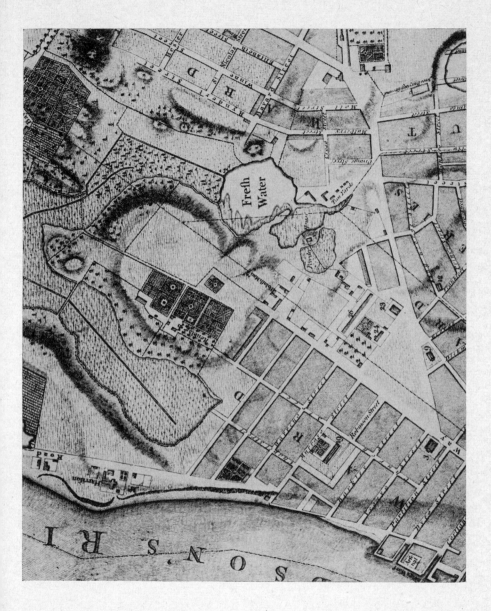

MAP 10

1782

A small local map of the Worth Street area.

The hospital is shown as "H." The Revolutionary War fortifications which surround it cover the area between Broadway and West Broadway and Leonard and Duane Streets.

A water reservoir is shown as "R," while another fort is shown to the left of the reservoir along the canal, now Canal Street.

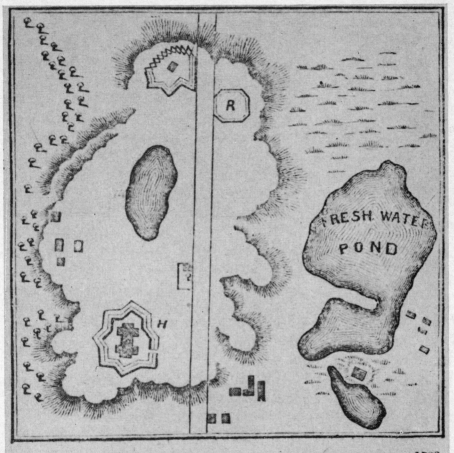

THE KALCKHOOK AT THE CLOSE OF THE REVOLUTIONARY WAR, 1782.

H. The Hospital fortified.
R. The Reservoir.

MAP 11

1783

This map shows the Revolutionary War fortifications in the Worth Street area. The hospital was fortified, and there were batteries near by on the Hudson, as well as a fortified line along Broome Street.

The city limit west of Broadway was at Chambers Street, which omitted the present Worth Street area, but to the east of Broadway the city extended to Grand Street.

This map shows the original size of lower Manhattan Island, while shaded portion shows the filled-in land which set the present shore line. The eastern shore of the island was filled in and extended out into the water from the old line at approximately Pearl Street. The first street on filled-in land became Water Street, then Front Street was added, and finally South Street. On the western shore, along the Hudson, Greenwich Street was near the original shore line. In time, during the filling-in process, Washington Street was added and later West Street.

The expansion of land area began with the coming of the Dutch. The first sailing ships arrived at the port to receive cargoes of furs and other items, but there being no great market at that time for Dutch imports, the ships arrived in ballast of rock, sand or bricks. There were no docks, so the ships simply anchored as near shore as possible and threw their ballast overboard. Thousands of ships arrived over the years, and this practice of dumping ballast continued into the English era. A new shore line began to form, with pockets and swamp lands between the rocky fill and actual shore.

As time passed on, the tides helped to fill in the spaces between the rocks and the shore, and to this was added the surplus rocks from leveling streets and material from the excavations for building foundations. Today there is a new shore line around the lower end of Manhattan from Canal Street to the Battery, on both rivers. The lower end of the island below City Hall is approximately twice as wide as in the Indian days, but about the same general shape. This filled-in land is now lined with docks and piers, and is some of the most valuable land in the city.

This building of the outer edge of the island is an episode all its own. The ships that brought to Manhattan's shores people from all nations of the world also brought actual parts of those nations in the form of rocks and sand, which were deposited to expand the shores of the island.

MAP 12

1789. The City Just After the Revolution

The New York Hospital, a vital part of Worth Street history, had been built in 1773, burned in 1775, and rebuilt in 1776. At that time it was stated that it was being built in the country north of the city.

By 1789 a few more streets had been laid out as the city continued northward. The old country road leading north of the City Hall to the hospital developed as a street as far as Leonard Street, and was named Great St. George's Street. There is a record that it was necessary to cut through a rocky hill at what is now Broadway and Worth Street, taking off twenty-five feet to achieve a fairly level grade. The waterway across the Island is clearly visible on this map as it flows east and west from the lake.

MAP 13

1797. A Local Map of the Worth Street Area

The hospital is shown, and the present Worth Street appears as Catherine Street. Thomas Street had not yet been cut through the hospital grounds. Leonard Street was the most northerly street. Church and Chapel Streets now extend to Leonard as more of the swamp has been drained.

The corner now No. 90 Worth Street was no longer part of the hospital, having been sold. The corner of Barley (Duane) Street and Broadway also was not part of the hospital grounds, as it was the site of the Anthony Rutgers home. The present Pearl Street was Magazine. At the right is shown Cross Street (Park) and Orange Street (Baxter), which, with the extension of Catherine (Worth) formed the Five Points.

Washington Street had been laid out along the Hudson. The Worth Street area is shown in the Sixth Ward.

MAP 14

1808

For the first time a map shows the streets completed through to the Worth Street area, from Chambers Street to Canal Street, which was on the edge of the swamp at the canal. Several of these streets had been laid out in 1789, and others in 1803. Streets had also been laid out about a half mile north of Canal Street, but the area was sparsely settled.

Catherine Street had become Anthony Street in 1803, and a portion of Collect Pond had been filled in, making possible the laying out of Elm Street, now Lafayette. Great George Street had become Broadway through the Worth Street area. The remainder of Collect Pond was filled in during 1808. The swamp has mostly been filled in and streets laid out as the city progressed northward.

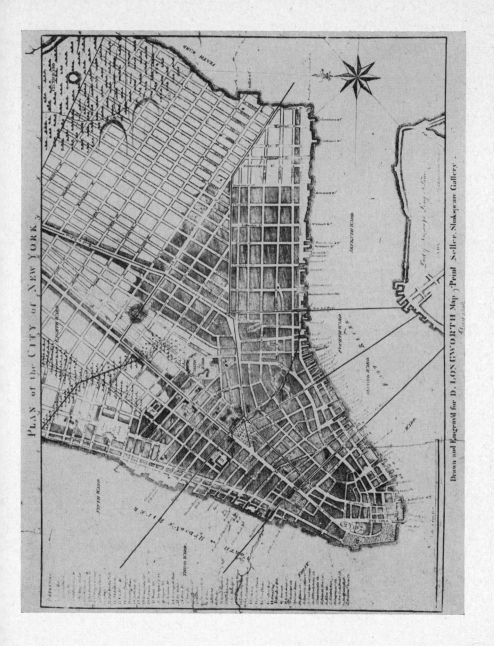

MAP 15

1808

This is a detail section of Map Fourteen showing the Worth Street area.

The hospital is shown on the map as No. 32, while No. 52 is the sugar refinery. No. 50 is the African Church, 54 the Universalist Church, No. 48 the Methodist Church, No. 58 the Congregationalist Church. Franklin Street is shown as Sugar Loaf. Church Street and Chapel Street now extended up to Canal Street. There was a rope mill east of the filled-in lake on Orange Street near White Street. The swamp was gradually diminishing in size as it was drained and filled in. The historic horseshoe was becoming citified.

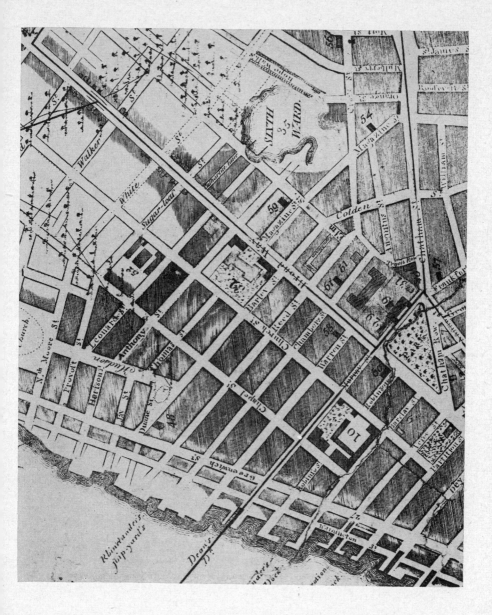

MAP 16

1853

This is one of a series of three maps, 16-17-18, which show the Worth Street area just 100 years ago when it had emerged as the textile center.

This map shows the section from Elm Street (Lafayette) to Broadway, from Leonard to Duane Streets by lot numbers, and also certain buildings that occupied these lots at the time. The Broadway Tabernacle Congregational Church, the Broadway Bank, the Broadway Theater, the Presbyterian Church and the Bowling Saloon, which had replaced the Masonic Temple, are shown.

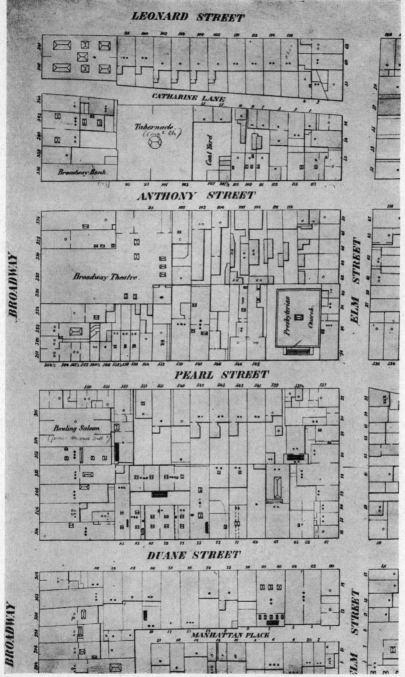

MAP 17

1853

The area between Broadway and Church Street, and between Leonard and Duane Streets is covered here.

Christ Protestant Episcopal Church is shown on lots No. 79-81-83 Anthony (Worth) Street. The layout of the New York Hospital is shown in detail. Part of the hospital property along Broadway had already been sold and cut into lots. There is a brewery on Duane Street.

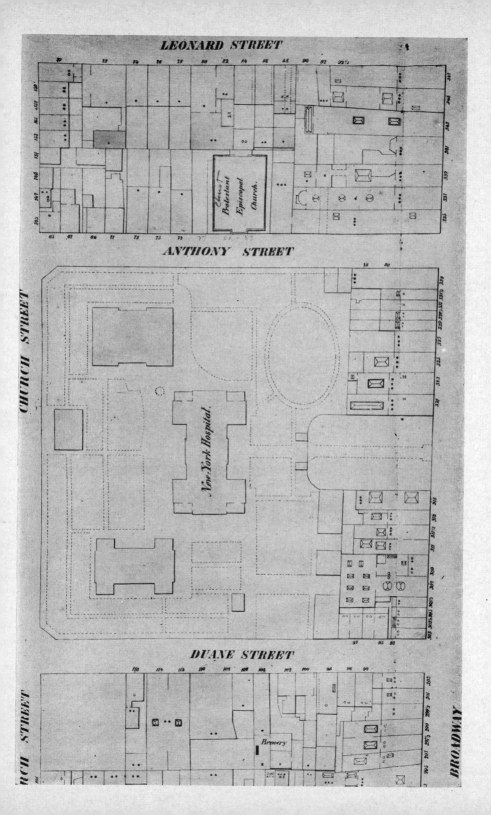

LEONARD STREET

ANTHONY STREET

DUANE STREET

CHURCH STREET

BROADWAY

Christ Protestant Episcopal Church.

New-York Hospital.

Brewery

MAP 18

1853

This map covers the area from Church Street to West Broadway and Leonard Street to Duane Street. The points of interest are: Zion African Methodist Episcopal Church, the Abyssinian Baptist Church, the Gas House, Public School No. 10, the Congress Steam Sugar Refinery and a Coal Yard.

5th & 6th Wards.

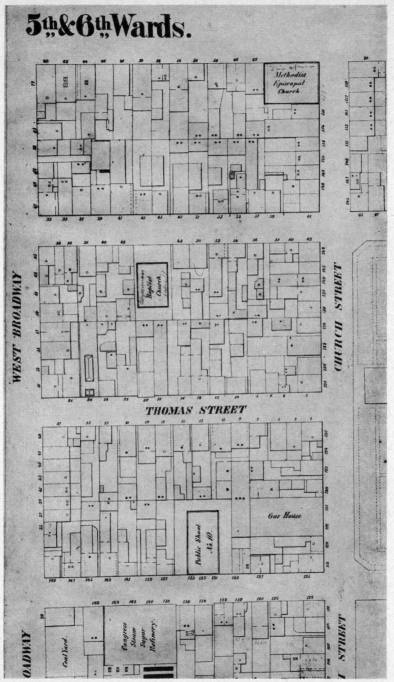

MAP 19

1865. A Resurvey of the Old Kalch-Hoek Farm

In preparing this map, the engineer said, "I find that Anthony Rutgers only conveyed 443 feet on the north side of the hospital and 432 feet on the south side and Church Street was intended to be 65 feet wide. I also find, by map on file, the block from Broadway to Church, on Worth Street, to be only 429 feet 8 inches, whereas it is 479 feet 8 inches. Allowing 25 feet to Church Street, we still have an error of 25 feet."

The old line between Kalch-Hoek and the Trinity Church property is shown near Reade and Church Streets. This line dates back to 1646.

The survey shows the hospital and lots which were sold along Broadway. Anthony Street is shown on both sides of the hospital, which is evidently an error, since Barley Street, now Duane, was on the south side.

The Sixth and Eighth Avenue Railroad was on West Broadway. This was chartered in 1851 to run from the corner of Barclay and Church Streets along West Broadway and Sixth Avenue to Fifty-Ninth Street. The Broadway and Central Park Rail Road was on Church Street.

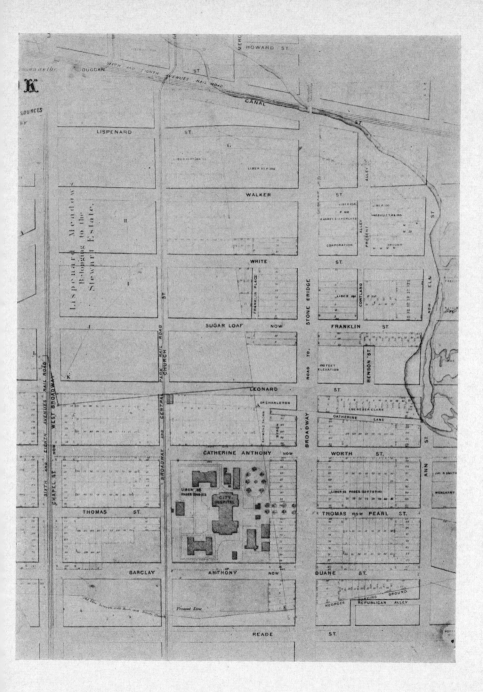

Pictures in the following pages, where not otherwise credited, are reproduced through the courtesy of The New-York Historical Society, New York City.

THE STORY IN PICTURES

Fortunately, some of the early pictures of Manhattan Island have been preserved. This makes it possible to illustrate the development of the island in a chronological manner that parallels the story in maps.

Some of the following illustrations have been taken from old drawings and sketches, others from photographs. Each represents an era in the history of Manhattan and the village of Worth.

The first picture represents a village of the Manhattes Indians. It is an artist's conception of an Indian longhouse and surroundings. Succeeding pictures shift the scene from the Indian village on the lake to the toe of the island, where the Dutch first settled. Later illustrations indicate the progress made during the Dutch and English eras, while others show the growth of the city northward until it reached the cite of old Manahatta.

Other pictures show early developments in Worth Village, and in some instances the names of firms who helped build the district. As indicated elsewhere, the Worth Street area has been the home of many industries, some of which had their start with only one or two firms. It has been at various times the center of the silk business, of wool, cotton, carpets, corsets, hosiery, lace, embroidery, underwear, shoes, clothing, shirts, as well as the printing, soap and perfume industries. The pictures from 1850 to 1900 indicate the wide range of businesses associated with Worth Street.

AMSTERDAM, een stedeken in Noord Amerikaes
View Nieu...op het eiland Manhattan, namaels Nieu york genaemt
van het gericht uit gebout der Engelschen

AMSTELODAMUM recens, nostra Anglis illud possidentibus
dictum Eboracum novum Nederlandiae novae, ut est Americae
Mexicanae sive Septentrionalis oppidulum

1673. A view of New Amsterdam about 1673 shows how close together the houses were built south of Wall Street. The "wall" may be seen at right.

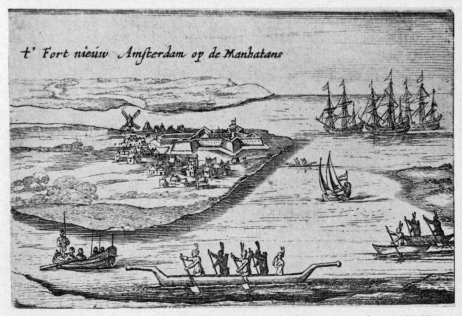

t' Fort nieūw Amsterdam op de Manhatans

1626. A crude sketch of the first Dutch settlement of New Amsterdam, 1626-28.

1679. The Stadthuys, the first City Hall on Manhattan, situated at what is now 73 Pearl Street.

1763. A view from near the present Worth Street area looking westward. In center background is the original Columbia College, which was on Church Street between Barclay and Murray Streets. The rugged terrain shows the difficulties encountered in laying out streets.

1800.   A view of old Manahatta Lake, known in this era as Collect Pond, after an etching made about 1800.

1785.   The famous Teawater Pump of English days on the site of the Indian Laughing Waters Spring. This sketch, made near the close of the Revolution, shows the Teawater men with their carts.

1816. The famous White Conduit House on Leonard Street between Broadway and Church Streets.

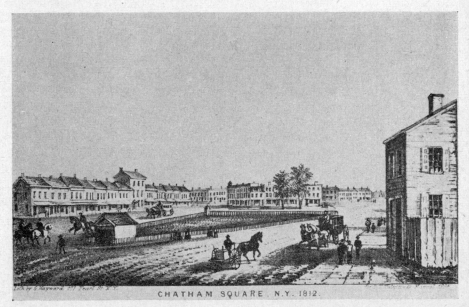

CHATHAM SQUARE, N.Y. 1812.

1812. Chatham Square, the eastern end of Worth Street.

1776. The second City Hall, located at Wall and Nassau Streets.

1807. A view of the famous New York Hospital when it was located in Worth Village. Thomas Street was later cut through from Broadway on a line approximately through the gate and center of the large building. The farthest right of the three buildings was on the corner of Worth and Church Streets, while the building farthest to the left was near Church and Duane Streets.

1812. The old stone bridge built over the canal (now Canal Street) when Broadway was extended. The old Stone Bridge Tavern and Garden are shown.

1826. Rutgers Medical College, built in 1826-27 on the south side of Duane Street east of Broadway.

1825. The water reservoir facing on Chambers Street. This reservoir, which extended north to Reade Street, was owned by the Manhattan Water Company, organized in 1800 to utilize the water supply of Collect Pond.

1826. The present City Hall, erected in 1815. This was the third City Hall on Manhattan Island.

1827. The infamous Five Points district at the intersection of Anthony (Worth) Street, Orange (Baxter) Street, and Cross (Park) Street. The Five Points area is now New York's civic center. '

1828. Contoit's "New York Garden" at Broadway and Leonard Street, as pictured in that year. It was opened in 1809, and soon became famous as a roadhouse and eating-place.

1828. South Street, as seen from Maiden Lane, bordering the original textile area near the Battery.

1830. The Masonic Hall at 314-316 Broadway, on the east side, looking south from the corner of Worth Street.

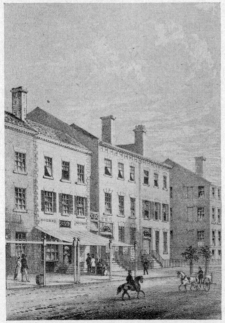

(*From a lithograph in* Valentine's Manual)

1831. Bourne's Store at 359 Broadway, near Franklin Street. This was the first, or one of the first retail dry goods stores in the Worth Street area.

1835. The great fire of December 16 and 17 of that year, as seen from the Bank of America Building, corner of Wall and William Streets. This fire burned out the textile merchants at the lower end of Manhattan, causing most of them to resettle ultimately in the Worth Street area.

1836. Broadway as viewed looking north across the Canal Street intersection.

1836. The National Theater, built in 1833, which stood on the corner of Leonard and Church Streets. It was destroyed by fire in 1839. It was first known as the Italian Opera House.

1844. Christ Episcopal Church, erected in 1822 at what is now 79-81-83 Worth Street, and demolished in 1853 to make way for business houses, as seen in 1844.

1841. The Broadway Tabernacle, erected at about this date. The domed building, which occupied 95-103 Worth Street, extended through to Catherine Lane, but its only entrance was at 340 Broadway. The columned building at left, 346 Broadway, housed the "Society Library."

(From a lithograph in Valentine's Manual)

1847. The Broadway Theatre, located at 326-330 Broadway and known as "Old Broadway," was a popular playhouse.

VIEW OF BROADWAY, N.Y.

(Courtesy of Durand Taylor)

1845. Near the corner of Broadway and Worth Street, with New York Hospital in the background. The Singer Building stood at 321-333 Broadway and 90 Worth Street. Note Fulton Ferry stagecoach at right, and Broadway-Fifth Avenue coach at left.

1847. A view down Franklin Street from a private home located at 367 Broadway.

1850. The famous Stewart Department Store at the northeast corner of Chambers Street and Broadway.

1850. Cooper House at Broadway and Worth Street.

(From an original lithograph owned by Durand Taylor and reproduced by permission)

1850. American sailing vessels of the 1850's were important textile consumers. Some of the famous clipper ships required seven thousand yards of cotton canvas for a suit of sails.

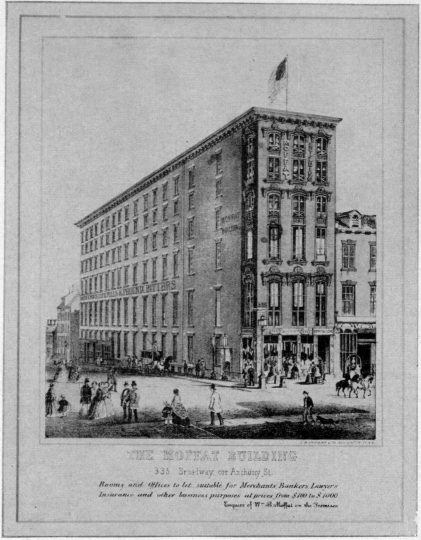

THE MOFFAT BUILDING

335 Broadway, cor Anthony St.

*Rooms and Offices to let suitable for Merchants Bankers Lawyers
Insurance and other business purposes at prices from $100 to $1000*
Enquire of W. B. Moffat on the Premises

1850. The recently erected Moffat Building at the corner of Anthony (Worth) Street
and Broadway. This was the headquarters of a flourishing patent-medicine business owned
by Dr. Moffat, who sold Life Pills and Phoenix Bitters. Note "To Let" announcement
beneath.

1850. The northeast corner of Worth Street and Broadway. The Broadway Bank is on the corner at 336 Broadway. The Tabernacle entrance is at 340 and the New York Society Library at 346.

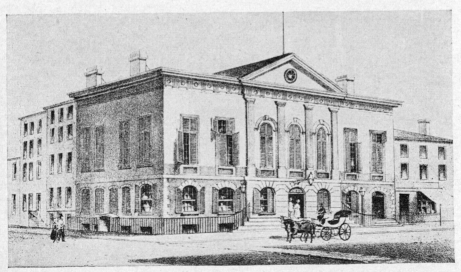

1853. Washington Hall, at the southeast corner of Broadway and Reade Street.

ENGRAVED BY J. SARTAIN

MAJOR-GENERAL WORTH.

1855. Major General William Jenkins Worth, for whom Worth Street was named in 1855.

1854. The Gem Saloon, a noted rendezvous at Broadway and Worth, and the political head-quarters of its day. It was fabulously decorated with private booths for those who wanted them.

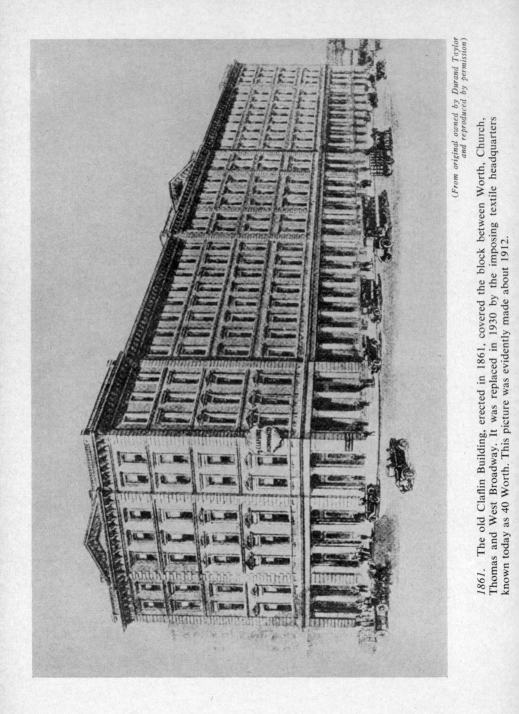

1861. The old Claflin Building, erected in 1861, covered the block between Worth, Church, Thomas and West Broadway. It was replaced in 1930 by the imposing textile headquarters known today as 40 Worth. This picture was evidently made about 1912.

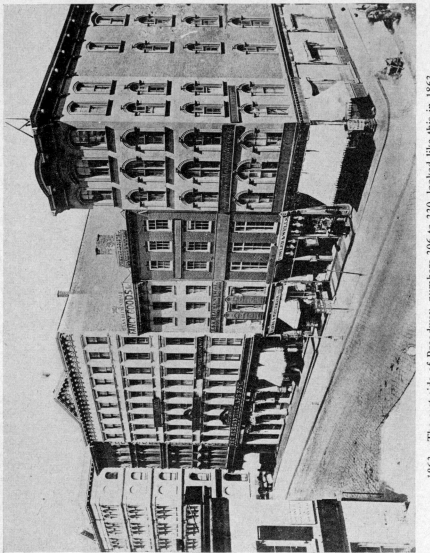

1863. The east side of Broadway, numbers 306 to 330, looked like this in 1863.

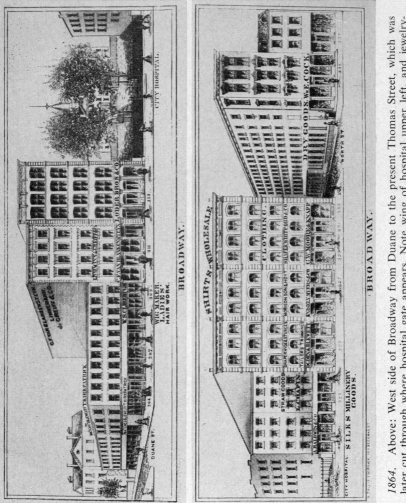

BROADWAY.

BROADWAY.

1864. Above: West side of Broadway from Duane to the present Thomas Street, which was later cut through where hospital gate appears. Note wing of hospital upper left, and jewelry- and wig-makers in the Worth Street area. Below: West side of Broadway from the present Thomas Street to Worth Street. As picture indicates, straw goods, silks, millinery, wholesale shirts and other clothing and dry goods were sold in Worth Street at this time.

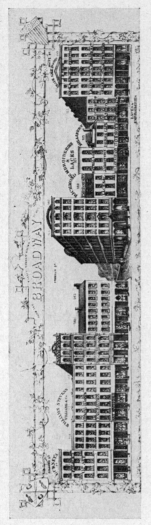

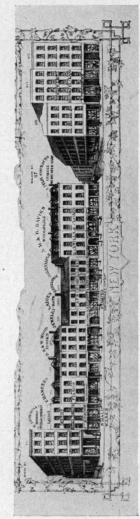

1864. Above: Broadway, west side, numbers 349 to 379, Leonard to Franklin to White Streets. Note the "Palace of Art." Looking-glasses, engravings, laces, embroideries, millinery, caps, books and printing were all part of the Worth Street business. Below: Broadway, west side, numbers 381 to 405, White to Walker to Lispenard Streets. Note that business in this area included publications, jewelry, books, pianos, caps, hats, cloaks, glass, china, dress trimmings and medicated soap.

1864. West side of Broadway, Chambers to Reade to Duane Streets. The Irving Hotel occupied numbers 273-287. Note window-shade, clothing, publishing and tailoring business in area.

1864. 5th Ward Hotel at West Broadway and Franklin Street.

SPIRAL OR CONTINUOUS WIRE SKIRTS.

SOLE MANUFACTURER OF PATENT.

LOCKWOOD SKIRTS CORSETS

G. W. LOCKWOOD

SKIRTS & CORSETS

C. W. LOCKWOOD

G. W. LOCKWOOD,
Nos 9 & 11 White Street. New York.

(*Courtesy of Durand Taylor*)

1865. Enterprising spirit of era is reflected in this old advertisement.

WORTH STREET NEW YORK

(From original owned by Durand Taylor
and reproduced by permission)

1865.   Worth Street in 1865 was a busy commercial district, as these drays and packing-cases indicate.

1867. The Hudson River Railroad Terminal at Chambers and Hudson Streets. The railroad, built in 1847, is now the New York Central. Horses drew the cars up Hudson Street, by Worth Street to Canal Street, to West Street and to Tenth Avenue, and thence to a terminal at Thirty-first Street.

A little-known picture showing Abraham Lincoln's funeral procession along Broadway in April 1865. It had left the City Hall and was passing Worth Street, going north. The caisson was at Leonard Street. The buildings were heavily draped in black, and the sidewalks crowded to capacity.

1872. Above: The original Merchants Club at 106-108 Leonard Street. Below: The present Merchants Club at 26 Thomas Street.

1877. East side of Broadway between Duane and Reade Streets. The Pattern Department of the *Ladies' Home Journal* occupied the building on the left. The middle building was tenanted by a manufacturer of horse collars, while another firm was a shirt manufacturer. On the lower floor was the Waterbury Brass Company.

1876. North side of Leonard Street west of Broadway. Kobbe & Ball, and Jaffe and Pincus, occupied one building.

1877. Worth Street, numbers 80-82-84-86. Firms shown include E. W. Holbrook & Co., Stursberg & Co., Thomson and Langdon. Corsets were sold at No. 84.

1877. Numbers 67-69-71 Worth Street, occupied by W. C. Peet & Co. and A. D. Juilliard & Co.

1877. Numbers 78-80 Worth Street. Four of the firms located here were Sulzbacher, Gitterman & Wedeles; W. C. Langley & Co., Holbrook & Co., Williston & Co.

1877. Numbers 69-71-73 Worth Street. Two of the occupants were W. C. Peet & Co. and Kibbe, Chaffee, Shreve & Co.

1877. South side of Worth Street between Hudson Street and West Broadway. Garner & Co. occupied the building, which was erected about 1875.

1877. Thomas Street between Church and Trimble Place. Wright, Bliss & Fabyan were doing business here. On the second floor front was the Engineer's Office of the Department of Docks, and at the right, C. H. Townsend.

1877. David S. Brown & Co. and Julian White occupied these premises at 95 Thomas Street.

1877. Numbers 350-352-354 Broadway, occupied by E. S. Jaffray & Co.

1877. Broadway at the northwest corner of Franklin Street.

1878. Numbers 68-70-72 Leonard Street, occupied by Blum & Weill, Wendell, Fay & Co., Haslehurst & Brother, and Frederick Vietor and Achelis.

1878. I. Frank & Co., York Street Flax Spinning Co., Klein & Hoexter, Stark & Lowenthal, Weil & Heidelbach and Isaac Rosenstein Co. occupied these buildings at 99-101-103-105 Franklin Street.

1886. East side of Broadway looking north from Worth Street across Catherine Lane and Leonard Street to Franklin Street.

1888. Broadway at Walker Street. Calhoun Robbins & Co., importers, occupied 408-410 Broadway.

Worth Street today. 40 Worth Street, the largest building in the area, rises above its neighbors in the textile district.

LISPENA
taken from the site of the
DRAWN BY